Wealth Creation Through Entrepreneurship

Dr. L. Venugopal Reddy Ph.D

&

Dr. P. V. Raveendra Ph.D

Professor, M.S. Ramaiah Institute of Technology, Bangalore.

Himalaya Publishing House

MUMBAI • NEW DELHI • NAGPUR • BENGALURU • HYDERABAD • CHENNAI • PUNE • LUCKNOW • AHMEDABAD • ERNAKULAM • BHUBANESWAR • INDORE • KOLKATA

Published by : Mrs. Meena Pandey
for **HIMALAYA PUBLISHING HOUSE PVT. LTD.,**
"Ramdoot", Dr. Bhalerao Marg, Girgaon, **Mumbai - 400 004.**
Phone: 2386 01 70/2386 38 63, Fax: 022-2387 71 78
Email: himpub@vsnl.com
Website: www.himpub.com

Branch Offices:

New Delhi : "Pooja Apartments", 4-B, Murari Lal Street, Ansari Road, Darya Ganj, New Delhi - 110 002.
Phone: 23270392, 23278631, Fax: 011-23256286

Nagpur : Kundanlal Chandak Industrial Estate, Ghat Road, Nagpur - 440 018.
Phone: 011-2738731/3296733, Telefax: 0712-2721215

Bengaluru : No. 16/1 (Old 12/1), 1st Floor, Next to Hotel Highlands, Madhava Nagar, Race Course Road, Bengaluru - 560 001.
Phone: 080-22281541/22385461, Telefax: 080-22286611

Hyderabad : No. 3-4-184, Lingampally, Besides Raghavendra Swamy Matham, Kachiguda, Hyderabad - 500 027.
Phone: 040-27560041, 27550139, Mobile: 09848130433

Chennai : No. 85/50, Bazullah Road, T. Nagar, Chennai - 600 017.
Phone: 044-28144004/28144005

Pune : First Floor, "Laksha" Apartment, No. 527, Mehunpura, Shaniwarpeth, (Near Prabhat Theatre), Pune - 411 030. Phone: 020-24496323/24496333

Lucknow : Jai Baha Bhavan, Church Road, Near Manas Complex and Dr, Awasthi Clinic, Aliganj, Lucknow - 226 024
Phone: 0522-2339329, 4068914,
Mobile: 09305302158, 09415349385, 09389593752

Ahmedabad : 114, "SHAIL", 1st Floor, Opp. Madhu Sudan House, C.G. Road, Navrang Pura, Ahmedabad - 380 009.
Phone: 079-26560126, Mobile: 09327324149, 09314679413

Ernakulam : 39/104 A, Lakshmi Apartment, Karikkamuri Cross Rd., Ernakulam, Cochin - 622011, Kerala.
Phone: 0484-2378012, 2378016, Mobile: 09344199799

Bhubaneswar : 5 Station Square, Bhubaneswar - 751 001.
Mobile: 9861046007, E-mail: orissa@himpub.com

Indore : Kesardeep Avenue Extension, 73, Narayan Bagh, Flat No. 302, IIIrd Floor, Near Humpty Dumpty School, Narayan Bagh, Indore (M.P.) - 452 007. Mobile: 09301386468

Kolkata : 108/4, Beliaghata Main Road, Near ID Hospital, Opp. SBI Bank, Kolkata - 700 010. Mobile: 09910440956

DTP by : HPH, Editorial Office, Bhandup (Shubhangi S.G)

Printed by : **7 Hills Printers,** Hyderabad.

PREFACE

"An average person works for others, an intelligent person works for himself" or "An intelligent person works for others, an average person works for himself". Which one is true? One who works for himself is an entrepreneur and one who works for others is an employee. In selecting the right choice for the above question, the idea of entrepreneurship was developed. Management community shall work for development of more number of employers than employees. **Wealth is respected everywhere in the world**. If one observes closely, all wealthy nations are those, who had more number of entrepreneurs. Somehow entrepreneurship is not a well developed and well respected profession in India. Poverty in India can be eliminated through entrepreneurship because by giving a fish to a hungry man, only one time, his hunger is mét, but, by teaching him fishing, hunger is removed in the long term. *An employee can fulfill the need of one family, where as an entrepreneur can fulfill the needs of many families and thus society.* Thus, this book is on "Wealth creation through Entrepreneurship"

We highlighted the qualities of entrepreneurs to know more about successful entrepreneurs. *"Leader makes the leaders and Entrepreneurs make the society."* Intelligence Quotient (I.Q.) gives a measure of what you can do and what you are capable of doing but Emotional Quotient tells you, what you will actually do. Entrepreneurship Quotient will tell what you have to do. Entrepreneurship: How to go about it?, highlights on the process of entrepreneurship. Entrepreneurship and innovation go hand in hand. The starting point of entrepreneurship is a new idea which comes from an innovation. New ideas and innovations emerge not only come from R & D but also from people. This include product innovations, process innovations, structural innovations, cultural innovations and supply chain innovations, etc. Well started is half done. Life is not full of roses; entrepreneurship is no exception to that. There is a special focus on problems of entrepreneurs and how to overcome it ethically are part of the business. Entrepreneurs can promote businesses successfully by practising ethics thus building relationship with customers. Hence, There lies the importance of ethics in entrepreneurship. People learn from Nature. We can also learn from movies.and our own experiances some interesting less ons from the movie *Munnabhai* are highlighted. There are more similarities between Intrapreneurs and Entrepreneurs than dissimilarities. In the global environment there are many opportunities for intrapreneurs as well as entrepreneurs. By practicing intraprenuership/entrepreneurship, one can explore the opportunities. To be more successful in an organisation, manager should act function as an intrapreneur. This book is meant for Management students, faculty, and budding entrepreneurs.

This book is about analogies, i.e., it gives stories in order to inspire people to start initiating the right approach to start an enterprise of their own. There are personal interpretation of the writer and to be taken in the context mentioned in the book wherever applicable.

Authors

CONTENTS

CHAPTER 1

Entrepreneurship: What is in it?

"The future belongs to not those who merely seek opportunity, but to those who create it."

Peter Drucker

One of the newspapers has recently highlighted that all IIM final year students are well placed with salaries ranging from Rs. 2000k to 8000k per annum. IIM Directors feel proud about their placements. The Directors of other reputed Institutes of Technology also are also proud that their students get 100% placement through campus recruitment with a package of Rs. 200000 to Rs. 800000 per month. If we keenly observe the above two cases one thing is common in both the types of Institutes. These Institutes are developing students who are ready and all set to work for others.

Why are these institutions unable to produce entrepreneurs? It might be the fear of failure by students or Institutes failed to inculcate entrepreneurial spirit in the minds of the students.

FEAR OF FAILURE

Many of us are afraid to do certain things because we fear that we may not prove out to be successful. The fear of failure prevents us from accepting and accomplishing great tasks. For the same reason, many talented people do not utilize their full potential. Entrepreneurs are no exception to that. The following story reveals the importance of team work in overcoming fear.

One day, Shyam was walking through a forest when he saw an eagle's egg lying on the way. He brought it home and kept it in the coop. The egg hatched and the little eagle grew up thinking that it was a chick. The eagle behaved exactly like the chicken. It scratched in the dirt for seeds and worms. It never flew more than a few feet as the chicken did. One day, the baby eagle saw an eagle flying in the open sky. It asked other chicken, "What bird is that? How beautiful it looks!". The chicken replied, "That is an eagle. You cannot fly like that because you are just a chick". One day, Shyam's friend visited him. He was surprised to see an eagle among the chicken. He asked Shyam why he had kept the eagle with chicken. Shyam told him the story why the eagle behaved like a chicken. The friend was surprised. 'How could an eagle behave like a chick," he thought. He said," It is an eagle. It can learn to fly. I will make it fly."

Shyam said," It will not fly because right from its birth it has been living in the company of the chicks". This friend was not convinced, "I will make it fly. Let me try. I am sure it would learn to fly," he said.

Shyam agreed and the visitor took the eagle in his arms and dropped it from a little height thinking that it would stretch its wings to fly. But the eagle did not fly.The next day, he took the eagle to the top of a building. When he was about to drop it, the eagle got frightened. It jumped out from his hands and joined the chicken. He tried for several days, but the eagle did not fly.

Finally, he took it to a place where there were many eagles. Seeing the other eagles flying, it got encouraged and tried to fly. At first, it flying could fly for a short distance. But after some time, it was ready to soar up in the sky. This time it stretch was ready to its wings and flew.

Like the eagle of this story, many of us are scared of failures. That is why we don't try. If we overcome the fear of failure, we will certainly be successful in our venture.

Many of us have potential to become entrepreneurs, but this fear of failure retreats us taking the first step makes us not take the first step in the right direction. In the above story, you can observe that, as long as the eagle was with the chicken, it failed to fly. The same thing happens in our families also, when a father is an employee, he wants his son also to become a better employee, but not an employer. He will directly or indirectly inculcate 'working for others' in the minds of his children. You can observe that in most of the cases an entrepreneur's son becomes an entrepreneur and employee's son becomes an employee. If you look at one of the richest states in India, *viz,* Gujarat, many people are employers and not employees. They create wealth through entrepreneurship.

Many of us do not venture into entrepreneurship because of our attitude and lack of will power.

ATTITUDE THAT MATTERS

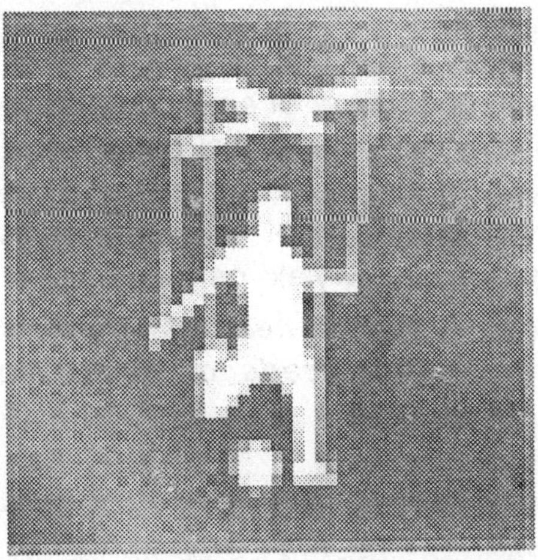

"The word impossible is found in the dictionary of fools."

Napoleon

Erik lost his vision at the age of 13, even then he managed to become an accomplishedathelet: Erik became the first blind man to climb Mt. Everest on 25th May, 2001. When he was 34 years old, he became one of the very few individuals to climb the highest peaks of all the seven continents.

Erik is a middle class school teacher and a wrestling coach. Added to this, he is a very good writer as well. He has received many awards. A few of them are Free Spirit Award, ESPN and ESPY award.

Most of us are blessed with everything in life yet we have not accomplished great things. What is the reason for this? It is because we lack will power and attitude. Successful Entrepreneurs have strong in will power to succeed.

Wealth Creation is Possible Only Through Entrepreneurship.

In India, we have maximum number of entrepreneurs. Surprised?

Yes, we have a maximum number of entrepreneurs but all of them are in the same profession? The farmers are good risk Agruculture takers compared to the many other people because they take risk with the monsoon. Despite a wide range of entrepreneurship in agriculture, wealth is not created due to low yield per hectore..

An employee can fulfill the need of one family, where as an entrepreneur can fulfill the needs of many families and thus society.

❒ ❒ ❒

CHAPTER 2 Characteristics of Entrepreneurs

ENTREPRENEURS ARE RISK TAKERS

"The trouble is, if you don't risk anything, you risk even more"

— Erica Jang

Entrepreneurs always take risk. Here is an example of a class room exercises in a Premier Management Institute.One of the Professors who teach 'Entrepreneurship management', while discussing in the class, wanted to know how many students were ready to take risk. He asked one student to bring a big basket and some hats. He kept the basket near the board and asked each of the students to throw the hat into the basket. All the students stood up at their respective places and tried their luck by throwing the hat into the basket. But one student walked to the basket and put the hat into the basket. Everybody was surprised including the Professor. The student answered with a smile 'entrepreneurs take risk, but they take risk when it is necessary. We were not asked to throw the hat into the basket from our respective places'.

ENTREPRENEURS ARE CREATIVE

"When nothing is sure, everything is possible."

— Margeret Drabble

Managers do not do different things, they do things differently.' This is one of the famous quotations from management guru, Shiva Khera (In the book 'You can win'). Entrepreneurs are supposed to achieve super ordinate goals with normal people. And to do this, they should be creative. Only then, they can achieve this. The following interesting incident happened in America and I have read it in newsletter of Quality Circle of Forum India, Bangalore chapter. In the Physics examination for 10 + 2 standard, a question was asked as to how to measure the height of the building using a barometer? A student had given four answers for the same and he failed in the examination. Then the student applied for revaluation, where the evaluator and the student sit together and value the answer script. The student was firm about his answer and the evaluator was also eager as only few scripts come had for revaluation. The evaluator read the answers written by the student and he was surprised. The answers were (1). Using the barometer as a scale first I will find the length of the barometer, and then using as scale I will find the length of the building. (2). I will go to the top of the building and drop the barometer. I will calculate the time required for the barometer to fall from top to bottom and using the usual distance-time formula I will calculate the height of the building. (3). On a sunny day, I will keep the barometer next to the building and find the length of the shadow of the barometer, and by comparing it with the length of the shadow of the building (as height of the barometer is already known)....... (4). I will go to the Engineer who constructed this building and I will offer the barometer to him if he can tell me height of the building. Then the Professor asked "other than these do you have any other solutions? Then the student answered "yes, I have one more solution which was told by my Physics teacher, measure the pressure at the ground level and at the top of the building using barometer and making use of the pressure difference one can find the height of the building." That is the level of creativity expected from the entrepreneur also. (If you have any other solutions for the question it is welcome because every problem has ten solutions.)

ENTREPRENEURS ARE GOOD LISTENERS

"The most important thing in communication is hearing what is not said"

— Peter F Drucker

In all MBA programmes there is a common paper on Communication Skills. Many a times, Personality development programmes offer training on communication skills. (According to one survey a manager spends 65% of his time on communication) The biggest challenge of communication is listening. We have many programs on delivery but unfortunately none on listening. But one of the important features of good communication is listening. (Even for a successful marketing executive, the most required quality is not to speak but to listen to what the customer says).

One day in a the de-addiction class, there was a big gathering. A Doctor wanted to demonstrate the ill effects of drinking alcohol. He asked for two jars one with plain water and one with alcohol. Then he put two earthworms into the jars. The earthworm which was in the plain water was swimming. The other one, which was in the alcohol jar, swam for some time and then died. Then the doctor asked a patient who was on the last bench 'What can be concluded from this experiment". The Patient replied "if we drink alcohol, worms in the stomach will die".

We are basically selective listeners. We listen to what we want and leave the rest.

Entrepreneurs are good listeners. They listen to everybody including customers, suppliers, employees and other then decide what to do.

ENTREPRENEURS ARE OPPORTUNITY SEEKERS

"A pessimist looks for a problem in every opportunity,

An optimistic looks for an opportunity in every problem"

In 1990s, when South East Asian countries economies collapsed all the MNCs in those countries either stopped investing or withdrew. To everyone's surprise Japanese started investing in those countries. The logic behind this was that-the yen became stronger than what it was before with respect to other currencies. They produced goods in those countries (by which the cost of production had became less) and exported to the rest of the world.

So every problem is an opportunity. When America put restrictions on Indian software products, we looked into the opportunities in the rest of the world.

This is an interesting story which I have picked from Akio Morita's book 'Made in Japan'. Akio's partner and friend Ibuka came to Akio's office with one of Sony's portable stereo tape recorders and with a pair of standard size headphones.. Ibuka looked unhappy and complained about the weight of the audio system. Then Akio asked about what was in Ibuka's mind. Then Ibuka replied " I like to listen to music, but I don't want to disturb others. I can't sit there with my stereo all the day. This is my solution what I have found. I take the music with me. But it is heavy".

The complaint of Ibuka generated a lot of thinking in Akio's mind. Then he developed the idea of Walkman. The rest is the history with the Walkman.

There is one interesting story in Swamy Sukhbodanand's audio cassette, which I am unable to forget over a long period of time. Madan Mohan Malveeya went to collect donation for Banaras Hindu University from a Mullah of Hyderabad who was against Hindus. The Mullah threw a chappal at Malveeya. Malveeya took the chappal (shoe) went to the market and auctioned it for a heavy price. After knowing the action of Madan Mohan Malveeya, Mullah sent the other shoe also to boost the price.

Aravind Netralaya of Chennai had shown the way how an eye surgery can be performed at Rs.1,000 without compromising on quality of operation.

Apollo Hospital has shown the way how a multi super specialty hospital can be run in an economically backward district (they are able to sell health consciousness among farmers, asking them to pay one rupee per day to UTI so that they will take care of the rest).

ENTREPRENEURS ARE RESPONS 'I' BLE

"No man will make a great leader who wants to do it all by himself, or to get all the credit for doing for it."

— **Andrew Carnegie**

Entrepreneur should accept responsibility. It is not simply acceptance of responsibility but he should be able to say "for all the success his subordinates are responsible and for the failures I am responsible". And not only saying but also practise it.

Let us go through the following real story shared by the ex-President of the nation in one of the interviews with CNBC. It happened in 1980 in ISRO, when Mr. Abdul Kalam was the Project Director and Mr. Kasturi Rangan was the ISRO Director. A satellite was supposed to be launched on a particular day and all the higher authorities came to Sriharikota to observe the great Indian feat. On the scheduled day at the scheduled time, the count down started. All the scientists were seated in front of the computers and were eagerly waching the progress. Suddenly there was an alert signal by the computer indicating a technical problem in the third stage of the ignition. Mr. Abdul Kalam who was in charge of the Satellite called an emergency meeting with the scientists and all of them suggested the project should go ahead as it is a very small problem (with an assumption that it will not affect the successful launching of the satellite). Now, Mr. Kalam had to take a decision as the machine says to stop the launching and the men (team) adviced to go ahead with the project. Mr. Kalam decided to go ahead with the project. The count down started 4..3..2..1.. the satellite started successfully from the ground with great lightening, there were smiles on all the faces, suddenly satellite changed it's direction and went directly to the Bay of Bengal. Every body was shocked. The Press were ready to attack with their questions as its cost was 20 crore rupees in those days. Mr. Kasturi Rangan called Mr. Kalam and said," Don't worry, I will meet the press". Mr. Rangan had a tough time with press people in answering them as the mission was a failure. After ten years, again the scientists worked day and night and the next launch was ready. Again all the higher authorities and press came to see the launch of the satellite. And this time, everything went successfully. Mr. Rangan called Mr. Kalam and said “Congratulation for the successful launching, well done, you go meet the press this time.” This is the way a entrepreneur has to accept the responsibility. One can observe that there is an ‘I’ in responsiblity. Entrepreneurs do not look for reasons but they accept the responsibility and focus on future solutions.

ENTREPRENEURS ARE DETERMINED

“Most of the important things in the world have been accomplished by people who have kept on trying when there seemed to be no hope at all.”

— Dale Carnegie

There are many examples that tell about the people who are determined. But our discussion will be restricted to one among them. This happened in Ford Motor Company in late 1960. The great entrepreneur Mr. Henry Ford decided to have 8 cylinders engine for the automobiles, a time when nobody could think of an 8 cylinder engine. He called his team of engineers and asked them to develop an engine with 8 cylinders. The team members were surprised and said “It is impossible”... But Ford said’, “No problem, you go ahead with the project.” One year passed there was no progress. Ford had a meeting once again with the team of engineers and they said again, “it is impossible.” Ford said “No problem, you go ahead with the project”. One more year passed away and there was no progress. The same episode repeated. Salaries were paid regularly to the team members without much contribution or development from them. After one more year, there was a break-through. They were able to develop an engine with 8 cylinders. The entire credit should go to Mr. Ford who was determined to develop an 8 cylinder engine. The 8 cylinder engine changed the face of the automobile industry and brought a lot of success to Ford Company.

Entrepreneurs have a positive attitude towards everything. They read 'impossible' as " I am possible". They do not have anything as impossible. They strongly believe that 'First I will do what is possible; and impossible can take a little longer".

ENTREPRENEURS KNOW HOW TO REACH THE GOAL

"Don't be afraid to take a big step when one is indicated. You can't cross a chasm in two small steps."

— David Loyd George

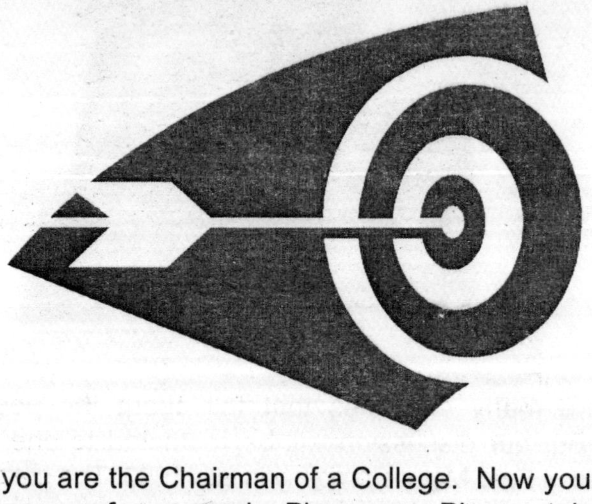

Imagine you are the Chairman of a College. Now you want to start a new course, say for example Pharmacy. Please take a piece of paper and list out your action plan.

Many of our answers will be like this. First, find the details about the requirements to start a Pharmacy College according to the statutory rules and regulations (check yourself whether it is possible to procure all the resources, if yes, go to second step). Second, procure all the requirements. And thirdly, apply for the statutory bodies for permission.

An experienced entrepreneur has a different style. First, he decides and applies for permission and before the inspection by statutory body, he will procure all the resources. One important point to be highlighted is that he is neither MBA nor a graduate (Of course, many management college owners are not MBAs). But he is simply a practising entrepreneur. There will be a lot of difference between "procure resources and decide" and "decide and procure resources". The difference is as simple as between 'employee' and 'employer'.

ENTREPRENEURS ARE GOOD AT NETWORKING

"In organization, real power and energy is generated through relationships. The patterns of relationship and capacities to form them are more important than tasks, and positions."

— Margeret Wheatly

The most important quality of Entrepreneurs is that they know how to deal with people and are very good in networking with people through out the day, i.e,. **24 X 7.**

Entrepreneurs are the people to bend the laws first, i.e., they want to make adjustment in rules and regulations.

As a Professor, one should be caring for front-line students while delivering lectures because they may be potential Professors to

teach new concepts. Also one should be caring for last-line students, as they may be potential donors to donate millions of rupees to your institution as they may be future entrepreneurs. If you are not convinced, it is right time to recollect some of the successful entrepreneurs without any formal education. Dhirubhai Ambani – college drop out, Bill Gates- college drop out, Henry Ford - high school drop out. Next time, you come across some of the successful entrepreneurs, just look into their educational qualifications, then you might accept my views. Entrepreneurs are more common sense oriented. Today, many MBAs are working for non-MBAs.

ENTREPRENEURS ARE BORN LEADERS OR MANAGERS?

"Leader makes the leaders
Entrepreneurs make the society."

In all MBA classes, the discussion on above topic is a heated one. Entrepreneurs are more *leaders than managers*. A manager *works for objectives,* whereas a leader *works for the purpose.* Studying MBA may be essential to be a manager but definitely for not to become a leader. You just look into the entrepreneurs who are around/known to you, definitely majority of them are not MBAs.

Somehow entrepreneurship is not a favoured profession in India. How many parents will encourage their children (after education) to become entrepreneurs?

ENTREPRENEURS EMPOWER THE PEOPLE

"An empowered organization is one in which individuals have the knowledge, skill, desire and opportunity to personally succeed in a way that leads to collective organizational success."

— Stephen R Covey

This is the information which I read in the daily 'THE ECONOMIC TIMES'. This is regarding the famous MTR (Mavalli Tiffin Room). In 1977, Janata Government declared regulation of food items. A control was imposed on the quantity and the amount of charges on the food items. MTR owners did not want to compromise on the quality and quantity because of price restriction. At the same time, they were not able to deliver the goods at the Government prices. So they stopped doing business. But the owner of the company continuously paid salaries to all the employees for six months even though there was no work for the employees. Employees wanted to reciprocate the gesture of the employer and set to think of a way to generate cash inflows for the company. Then they started making food mixes and pickles in the brand name of MTR and started selling door to door. The business of MTR pickles and powders picked up slowly. Even after the controls were removed, MTR continued to do business in pickles and MTR proved its leadership in the market. Today, MTR is one of the market leaders in pickle industry. Entrepreneurs know how to empower their employees. They practice the following Chinese proverb.

"If you plan for a day, plant corn,

If you plan for months, plant trees,

If you plan for a decade, plant men."

Planting men is possible through empowering.

GAIN STRENGTH THROUGH FAILURES AND ACHIEVE SUCCESS

"You may have a fresh start any moment you choose, for this thing that we call 'failure' is not the falling down but the staying down."

— Mary Pickford

Abraham Lincoln was a great failure as a student, as a lawyer and even as a legislator initially. But his success was largely due to his commitment to the mission. We saw him as a powerful leader. Similarly, failures recharge entrepreneurs and move them to the realm of success. Abraham Lincoln won only one election in his life time, i.e., as President of USA (before that he was defeated in all the elections which ever he contested). Edison failed 99 times before inventing the bulb. Entrepreneurs do not become bitter with failures, but better and better.

"Failare is Pillar of Succes"

SELECT THE RIGHT PEOPLE

"People make or break the organizations."

The toughest job for an entrepreneur,is the selection of right person for the right job.

If you are an Human Resource Manager and you are in the selection committee, whom do you select between Mr. A: who is highly skilled with poor attitude and Mr. B: who is averagely skilled with good attitude (Always better to select a person who has right attitude).

It is correct to say that a right person in a position is an asset and the wrong person is a liability to the organization.

ENTREPRENEUR KNOWS HOW TO RESOLVE CONFLICTS

"The significant problems we face cannot be solved at the same level of thinking we were at when we created them."

— Albert Einstein

In many companies, we see that there will be hire and fire policy. If you ask why they are fired, the company people say that it is because of difference of opinions and ideas.

Let us learn from Akio Marita (Sony) how to deal with when you have different opinions.

Once, there were different opinions on a particular item between Michiji Tajima, Chairman of board and Akio, deputy president. One day, Tajima told Marita, "You and I have different ideas. I think it is right time for me to quit" Then Akio told: "Sir, if you and I had exactly the same ideas on all subjects, it would not be necessary for both of us to be in this company and receive a salary. Either you or I should resign in that case. It is precisely because you and I have different ideas that this company will run a smaller risk of making mistakes."

Mr. Tajima continued in the company.

ENTREPRENEUR TAKES A CHANCE

"Luck favours only those who take a chance."

'We're in luck— we've discovered a new species!'

Many of us think that entrepreneurs are lucky. No, they got luck because they have taken more risks than others. Let us see the success story of Mr. Bill gates.

The product launched by Microsoft into its leadership position in the software industry was MS-DOS, the operating system for IBM and IBM compatible personal computers. The original DOS program, however, was not developed by Microsoft but by a company called Seattle Computer, where it was known as Q-DOS (which stood for 'quick and dirty operating system') What happened was, when IBM was looking for an operating system to run its original PC, it contacted a number of software companies, including Microsoft, asking them whether they could develop such a system. IBM did not, however, get in touch with Seattle Computer. Bill Gates, as a player in the emerging Seattle computer community knew that Seattle Computer had already developed a disk operating system. Gates borrowed $50,000 from his father, a senior partner in a prominent Seattle law firm. He then went to see the CEO of Seattle Computer and offered to purchase the rights to the company's Q-DOS system. He did not, tell them that IBM was looking for a disk operating system. Since Seattle Computer was short of cash, the CEO quickly agreed. Gates renamed the system as MS-DOS, some what upgraded , and licensed it to IBM. The rest, as they say, is history.

So was Microsoft lucky? Of course, it was. It was lucky that Seattle Computer had not heard about IBM's request. It was lucky that Gates knew about Seattle Computer's operating system. And it was lucky that IBM approached Microsoft. It was lucky that Gates knew about Seattle Computer's operating system. And it was lucky that Gates had a father wealthy enough to lend him $ 50,000 at a short notice. On the other hand, to attribute all Microsoft's subsequent success to luck would be wrong. While MS-DOS gave Microsoft a tremendous head start in the industry, it did not guarantee that Microsoft would continue to enjoy the kind of worldwide success that it has. Microsoft had to build the appropriate set of resources and capabilities required to produce a continuous stream of innovative software, which is precisely what Gates did with the cash generated from MS-DOS. The creativity asset pooled in by Gates brought success to him.

ENTREPRENEUR CAN FIND AN OPPORTUNITY IN EVERY PROBLEM

Entrepreneurs never accept defeat, they accept failures and work on them and become successful. I hope all of you might have heard the success story of Mr. Kurian Varghese, when he was insulted in one of the IIM board meetings; he founded Indian Institute of Rural Management. If Mr.Kurian had *chaltahai* attitude today, there would have been no IIRM. One of the banks did not accept the cheque signed in Telugu by Pattabi Sitaramaiah, a great freedom fighter. He went and started Andhra Bank. If Mr. Pattabhi Seethramaiah had *chaltahai* attitude today there would have been no Andhra Bank. Successful entrepreneurs have this "fight back" attitude. Entrepreneurs can find an opportunity in every problem.

ENTREPRENEURS ARE PROACTIVE

"Life is change. Growth is optional. Choose wisely."

... Clark

CHANGE IS CHANGING. All of you might have heard of this story when you were in school. A hat vendor who was going through a forest took rest under a banyan tree. While taking rest, he slept for some time. When he got up, he observed that all the hats were taken away and worn by the monkeys. He had only one hat on his head. He did not know how to get back the hats from the monkeys. Then he waved his hand, all the monkeys also waved their hands, then he clapped, all the monkeys also clapped.......and the rest is the story. Many of us know this the story up to there. But the real story for management students starts only now... As in many family businesses, his son also becomes a hat vendor. He told the entire story to his son. Accidentally, the hat vendor's son also came through the forest and he happened to take rest under the same banyan tree. When he woke up he saw all the hats were with the monkeys but not in his bag He recollected the story told to him by his father. He waved his hand; all the monkeys also waved the hands. When he clapped, all the monkeys also clapped. Then he threw his hat, the monkeys did not throw their hats. They told the vendor, "Hey, fool, not that you alone have a father, but even we have."

If you are not updated, you are outdated. Nobody wants to buy outdated medicine.If you are update you can market yourself better In the same way, irrespective of whether we are entrepreneurs or intrapreneurs we will have to update ourselves. A candidate who wants to become an employee in a company has to first market himself (may be only once) at the time of interview. But a candidate who wants to become an entrepreneur has to market many times or forever (first to family members, financiers, employees, suppliers, customers etc.)

ENTREPRENEURS ARE COMMON SENSE ORIENTED

"Common sense is not commonly available."

In the past, successful entrepreneurs did not study any management course, but they were able to achieve the goals with common sense. It is very tough to teach common sense in the class rooms. This is one of the reasons why many students after doing their MBA still are unemployed. If you are not convinced, please go through this. Mr. Shine after successfully completing his MBA with Finance specialization attended an interview in a Leasing Company in Hyderabad (which gives vehicles on lease). The interviewer after asking the personal details, put a question with respect to leasing. He asked, a If customer asks for a lorry (on lease) for transportation of tomatoes from Hyderabad to Mumbai will you give the lorry on lease or not?". (If you were in the same position what would be your answer). Mr. Shine thought for some time and replied "if there is a demand for tomatoes in Mumbai, and the customer credit worthiness is good,. I will give the vehicle on lease." The interviewer said "O.k., I will inform you later about the results". Mr. Shine came to his home with lots of hope, and shared his experience with his family members. His brother, who had failed to complete graduation heard this and said, "You will not get this job, because the interviewer's motto was to find out not about the credit worthiness or demand at that particular place, but he wanted to check if you were ready to provide the vehicle for perishable goods or not." I hope all can guess the outcome of the interview. After hearing the above episode from my friend, I used to put the same question to the MBA students and all used to give the same answer like Mr. Shine. It is very tough to teach common sense in the classrooms. And common sense is the basic requirement for any entrepreneur.

The irony of common sense is that it is not commonly available. My father used to ask me when I was a child, "There are 100 crows sitting on a tree. A gunman shoots one crow on the tree many crows are left over?"

There was Mr.Ranga, 29 year old (bachelor) who had failed in 8th standard wanted to start his own factory. He wanted to take a loan from State Financial Corporation under unemployed youth scheme. But, SFC lends funds only to those who have passed minimum 10th standard. If Ranga wanted to avail loan under this scheme, he had to pass 10th standard, which would have taken another one or two or three years for him and thus he had to postpone his business plan for a few more years. Many people were sure about his commitment and eagerly waited how Ranga would come out of this problem. Ranga got the loan within three months. Can you guess 'How it was possible?'. He married a girl who had completed 10th standard and got sanctioned loan from SFC in her name. Entrepreneurs look for solution with their common sense.

ENTREPRENEURS ARE TACTFUL

"If you have a lemon, make lemonade."

— Howard Gossage

We may confuse strategy with tact. Here is an example to understand what you mean by tact. Family oriented businesses are very common in India. A cloth merchant Mr. Ram Kuber had three sons. He had a big showroom in the market. He became old; he called his sons and told them to equally share the business. The three sons decided to divide the showroom and make three parts of it. All of them wanted to start the same business. The first son started the business in the name of "Kuber & sons". Second son named his showroom as "Kuber & brothers". Third son, who was also in the same business, was left without a name. He thought for a while and put the board "Entrance".! That is what tact means. Entrepreneurs should be strategic as well as tactful.

Mr. Vijay Mallya suggested Kissan food to introduce jam in small bottle (rather than in kg), Kissan foods introduced jam in small packets and made huge sales. The concept of packing in sachet started with Chik shampoo. Now it may not be surprising that anything is available in small sachets particularly consumer goods.

ENTREPRENEURS RESPECT EVERYBODY

"Don't think that because you are at the top you can boss over others around. Be very clear on what you have decided to

do and what you ask others to do and take full responsibility for it. Scolding subordinates and looking for people to blame for problems — seeking scapegoats — is useless. It is better to make use of motivation to accomplish something that will be to the advantage of both."

— AKIO MORITA

Who is important in the organisation?. Is it lower level employees or higher level employees? This is an interesting story from the Panchatantra. There was a rat in the forest. One day, it saw a lion sleeping near a tree and started playing on the lion. The lion got up saw the rat playing on its back; and was furious. It was ready to kill the rat, when the rat said, "Please forgive me; I may be helpful to you some day." The lion was surprised by the rat's words. The lion thought for a moment, "This rat is so small creature in comparison to me, how would it help me in the future, still I will let it free." One day, a hunter laid a net in the forest, and the lion was trapped in the net and was helpless. The rat saw the fate of lion; and it immediately jumped into the task, cut the net into pieces using its sharp teeth, and helped him get free.

There is nothing like important employees in the organisation. Every one is important for the organisation. (It does not matter whether he is at a higher level or a lower level).

If you enter into any organization, the first person you come across is a receptionist. If he/she shows an arrogant behaviour, we form a negative opinion about the entire organization and not only about him/her. Because, the organization is nothing but a pool of human resources. Long back, BPL Company rightly recognized the importance of this and put the first marketing executive of the company as its receptionist and trained on 'how to smile'. (First impression is the best impression).

ENTREPRENEURS ARE CUSTOMER ORIENTED

In 1980s, an Indian business executive who was on a trip to Tokyo, Japan, bought a tape-recorder from a Sony showroom. When he came back to his hotel and switched on the tape-recorder; to his surprise it did not work at all. He had no time to go back to the showroom and as his flight was scheduled within an hour. He called the Sony showroom and informed that the tape-recorder, which was purchased an hour before, was not working properly and he did not have sufficient time to personally return the tape-recorder. The business executive thought, whatever amount he spent on the tape-recorder was a waste. After one-hour, he took the flight to Bombay. When he came out of the security check up in Bombay airport, a person was standing with a placard with his name. The business executive met the person and introduced himself. To his surprise that person was a Sony sales executive. He said, "Thank you for buying our Sony tape-recorder, and sorry for the inconvinience it caused by not working properly. Here is a new one, please take this new tape recorder of the same model that you bought in Japan. We will not allow any defective unit to be delivered to the customers." You may realise how Sony is committed to the customers. (If anyone thinks for two minutes, he can understand how they are able to replace a defective unit, i.e., bought in Japan, with the new one in Bombay). Sony might have spent considerable amount in doing the above job. But it won the customer's heart permanently. Sony had done this because they strongly believe and practice excellence and superior performance in each and every aspect. They want to maintain long-term **relationship** with the customers. Entrepreneurs are aware that a good mouth will tell to 3 customers and a bad mouth will tell 11 customers.

ENTREPRENEURS ARE RATIONAL

"A leader has to be practical and realistic, yet must talk the language of a visionary and the idealistic."

— Eric Hoffer

Let us consider an example related to the corporate world. G E Home Appliances observed the family patterns in the world. They found that there were more no. of individual small families than joint families. So they thought that with the reduction of the family size (husband, wife and two children) the size of the homes will decrease and there will be a lot of demand for small size equipment in the kitchen also. They introduced small size kitchen equipment in the market. To their surprise, the sales did not pick up. The main reason for it was the fact that there will not be much change in the size of the kitchen with the number of family members. Housewives agree to reduce the size of all the rooms in the home except the kitchen (hence kitchen equipment). The company was forced to introduce the normal size of kitchen equipment.

Similar type of situation arose when Sony's Akio wanted to introduce walkman in the USA. In the USA, the houses are very big, and naturally, they like big things. The size of the walkman was small. But Akio thought logically, even though the room sizes are big, each one wants to listen to different types of music, and the walkman also offered mobality So he took the decision to introduce the walkman in the USA. It was a big success.

ENTREPRENEURS HAVE CONVINCING CAPABILITY

"Understanding human needs is half the job of meeting them."

— Adlai Stevenson

Many of us have strong beliefs about change. Some people change easily, some people will change with difficulty, and some people never change. This belief may be because 'old habits die hard'. This story was told by my uncle. One day, Sree Krishnadevaraya got some unique thought about the eating habit of goats. A goat continuously eats grass and does not stop eating as long as it is available. Sree Krishnadevaraya called Tenali Ramakrishna and said 'I will give you three months time and you should show that when grass is offered to a goat, it should refuse it. If you do the job, you will be rewarded with handsome quantity of gold or else you will be hung." Tenali had no other choice but to accept the challenge. He bought a goat, and lot of grass. He started giving big quantities of grass to the goat. At the end of the day, the goat was still eating it. Tenali was fed up with the goat and two months had passed away with no solution in sight. He became dull day by day as the dead line approached. His son observed the frustration on his father's face and he asked him the reason. Tenali explained the entire story to his son. His son said, 'I will do the job, just go and buy some more time from the King." King accepted to give some more time. Every day, the son used to take the goat outside the house and used to offer a lot of grass to the goat. Then he used to bring the goat inside the house. Again he used to offer grass with one hand and had a stick in the other. When the goat tried to take the grass, he used to hit the goat on its mouth. He used to do the same job everyday. The goat was conditioned in such a way that it began to realize eating inside the house will bring beating whereas eating outside will not. So, I should not eat grass inside the house. Now the training was completed. The Son took the goat to the palace and told the King that he was ready to prove what was required. The King ordered a good quality of grass and asked Tenali's son to offer the grass to the goat. The son took the grass in one hand. He had the same stick with him clearly visible to the goat. Then he offered the grass to the goat. Eventhough it was a good quality of grass, the goat could see the stick and did not accept the food. The King was surprised and honoured Tenali with the assured quantity of gold. Thus, we can change the people with the convincing skill. But each problem requires different types of convincing skills.

ENTREPRENEUR KNOWS HOW TO ADD VALUE

Coffee powder is generally packed in colourful packages and there is no value added to it. In one village, a local coffee manufacturer thought for a while and observed there was no value addition in the packing. Then, he started selling the coffee powder in steel tins instead of plastic covers for the same price. It was a big success. Soon, the steel containers became a common sight in almost all the houses in several villages. **Entrepreneurs always think how to add value to the product in every activity they do.**

ENTREPRENEURS LEAD BY EXAMPLE

" Unless commitment is made, there are only promises and hope...........but no plans."

— Peter Drucker

Recently, I was waiting outside a vegetable market while my wife was busy in purchases. As my vehicle was parked near a fruit vendor, I was observing his sales proceedings. That seller seemed to be a farmer, rather than a merchant. A customer came and bought all the fruits from the vendor, and he was asking for more. There was a small packed bag of fruits. Customer asked to sell those fruits also to him. But the vendor was reluctant to sell those fruits. The customer was surprised and asked why. The vendor said, "One customer bought these fruits half an hour back since he did not have change, he said he will come back with the change." Then the customer said, "If half an hour is already passed, he may not come back and afterwards you may not find a customer for these fruits." Then the vendor said, "I would wait for another half an hour, if he does not come I will not sell these fruits to any one, but I will take it to my home and give it to my children." I was astonished to see the vendor's commitment towards the customers. Customer commitment cannot be taught in sales training programmes. It should be shown through practice. Entrepreneurs should be committed towards customer service.

ENTREPRENEURS CONCENTRATE ON LONG-TERM BENEFITS

Many of the management professionals and students have heard the following in their first marketing management or sales management classes. A customer entered to buy a fan at a fan dealer's shop. The newly appointed salesman who was attending this enquiry (even though, he knows there is no stock) says to the customer, "There is no stock but the one special piece available is not for sale." The customer asked him with anxiety what was special about the piece. The Sales executive replied that the company has a policy to make separate fans for its' dealers with ball bearings inside which will have 3 years life more than normal one and such one is for being fitted in the dealers room and it is not for sale. A lot of interest was generated in the customer by the way sales executive presented to him. Now, the customer was interested in buying that fan and asked for it. Then, sales executive told that he had to take special permission from his superiors for selling that one..... And the rest is story. This is a good example for selling and was too good on that day but, not everyday. Because the sales executive made **one** sale and lost **ten** permanently.

Successful entrepreneurs look for long-term benefits rather than short-term benefits. Generally, many organisations decide what to do first and then look for people. But great companies decide on people first and look for what to do. Successful organizations are built by great people.

KNOW HOW TO CONSERVE THE RESOURCES

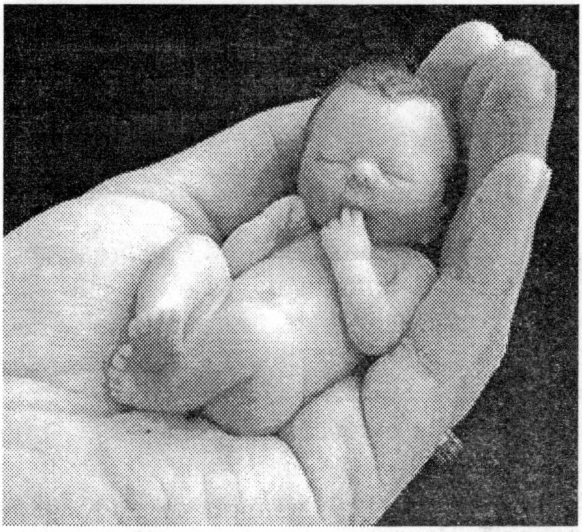

There are different ways to conserve your materials. Many a timewith a little bit of effort you can do the same. One such strategy was followed by WIPRO FLUID POWER which is strategically located in Andhra Pradesh in Hindupur, Anantapur District, which is economically backward district and is only 90 km away from Bangalore. The principle which was practised by the materials manager is that nothing should be kept on the ground. Quality of items will deteriorate when they come in contact with foreign particles like water, dust, chemicals which are used to clean the floor. This can be avoided by keeping them on a frame (wooden or metal). In this factory, all the raw materials are kept on wooden frames.

ENTREPRENEURS BELIEVE IN THEMSELVES

"A good leader inspires people to have confidence in the leader. A great leader inspires people to have confidence in themselves."

One of the TQM gurus visited India and was preaching the concept of 'doing it right first time and every time' at one of the training programmes in Bangalore. One from the audience asked him "many times you will be doing the job first time and how it is possible to do it right." Very interesting question! The answer is also is very interesting, the TQM guru replied, "it is practically possible to do it right first time and every time, provided you have an intention to do it. Let me ask a very simple question: How many times has your hand taken the food to the nose while eating? How many times you put your right leg into the left shoe while wearing the shoes?" ... So, doing it right first time and every time is possible provided you have an intention to do it.

TAKES THE JOB SERIOUSLY

"To be a leader, you have to make people want to follow you, and nobody wants to follow someone who does not know where he is going."

One of the Indian Companies decided to go for TQM implementation. It had made arrangement for one week training programme with one of the Japanese Gurus and one fine day the training programme started. In the training programme, all top and middle level managers, including CEO were attending. After half an hour of the training programme, CEO got a call and he left the Training Hall. After 5 minutes, TQM guru stopped the training programme and said, "if the top management is not committed towards TQM, there is no meaning in continuing the programme, I am going to cancel this programme and you need not pay the fee for this programme." And he left the place.

ENTREPRENEURS SHOW CONSISTENCY IN BEHAVIOUR

"What is character but determination of the incident?"

What is incident but the illustration of character?

— Henry James

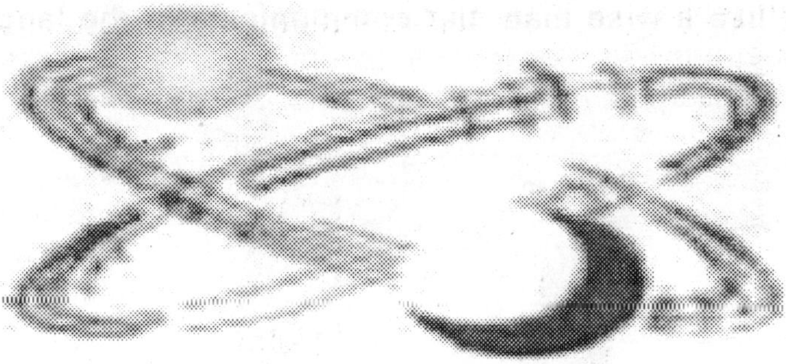

There was an employee, Mr. Genuine who named him self to be very truthful and honest. One morning, he went to the market and bought vegetables for Rs.7. He gave a ten rupee note, the seller by mistake returned one rupee extra, i.e., four rupees instead of three rupees. Mr. Genuine counted it and thought for one minute and returned the extra rupee. Then he went to a provisions shop and bought an item which costed eighty rupees. He gave a hundred rupee note and in return the seller gave three ten rupee notes. Mr. Genuine was surprised and counted it once again and thought for one minute (thought about his principles) and gave ten rupee note back. He went back home. To pay rent to the house owner he gave three five hundreds rupee notes (Rs.1500). The rent for his house was only 1200 rupees only. By mistake, the owner also gave four hundred rupee notes back (Again one hundred Rupees note extra). This time he thought for a longer time (about his principles) and returned the hundred Rupees note back. He went to the office from where he went to the bank to withdraw some amount from his savings account. He wanted to withdraw Rs.10, 000 from the bank. The Cash counter was very busy. As it will a Public Sector Bank, as usual it took 20 minutes for his turn to come. As the cashier was busy, by mistake he gave eleven thousand Rupees notes to Mr. Genuine. Mr. Genuine counted it twice, thrice. And was sure that he received one thousand Rupees note extra (eleven instead of ten). He did not think too much this time about his principles. He observed that Cashier was busy with his work. Mr. Genuine walked out of the counter.

I don't now whether all of us are like him or many of us are like him or few of us are like him. (Please check your self, whether you are like him or not. Be honest with your answer. That is the reason we made a separate chapter on 'ethics' in this book).

Communicate Properly the Mission of the Company

"Think like a wise man, but communicate in the language of

the people."

Many companies have very detailed mission/vision statements. But only few companies are able to communicate it clearly to their employees. I had come across one such experience while collecting data for my Ph.D. (CRM in financial services with special reference to leasing in Bangalore, Karnataka). I had taken an appointment with one of the regional sales managers at 5.00 p.m. for the data collection. I was there at sharp 5.00 p.m. in front of the office at Bangalore. I walked in and enquired about the regional sales manager with the receptionist. She said, the manager was not in the office and he would come back in an hour. I had no other option but to wait for the RM. While I was sitting there I heard a person having a high pitched conversation with the security guard. According to the instruction given to the Security Guard, no customer should be allowed inside after five. But the customer being employed elsewhere could visit the bank after attending his duties. He contacted the Receptionist through intercom (phone) and she asked the Security Guard to allow him inside. I was surprised by the way the Security Guard dealt with the customer. One hour passed. I went and enquired with the Receptionist about my appointment with the manager. Then she took two minutes on the phone and replied that he was not available. I was shocked because I called up the Regional manager at 4.00 p.m. and confirmed my appointment. The receptionist allowed me to make call after a request. I called up the RM's mobile and informed him about my appointment and then he spoke to the receptionist. After two minutes, to my surprise, she told, "Sir is inside, go and meet him." He received me well and we had a half an hour discussion about my thesis. Some of the highlights of our discussion are listed below.

- Our BANK (name of the bank is not mentioned intentionally) is the first bank to implement CRM (Customers Relationship Management) in India.
- But many of the executives and lower level employees are not involved in it. Many of them are not aware of it.
- They think of CRM more as software package than a strategy for the bank.
- Employees are not trained for the CRM implementation.

I thanked the receptionist also. On the way back, I asked the Security Guard about the material he was reading. He replied, "Sir, I am preparing for M.A. second year examination." (His rude behaviour might be because of his under-employment)

I came out of the bank; I met the same customer who had a quarrel with the Security Guard. He looked very annoyed. I went to him and asked "What is the problem?'. He replied gently, "Sir, I had taken a loan from the bank one year back. I repaid the principal and interest two months back. But, the house property documents which I had pledged as surety for the loan I had taken have not been returned. It has been pending for the last two months. Whenever I call up, I am told that the documents are in the Head Office, Mumbai and it is in the process of being returned. If I have to come here during day time I have to apply for casual leave. This is my fifth visit and I have made 20 to 30 calls. Here, no one takes responsibility and I am told that the concerned person is not available or he is too busy. But I am not interested in them; I want to get back my documents. They show a lot of interest while sanctioning the loan, but the same interest is lacking after I paid back the loan. I have never come across such service with any other bank in my life."

All this happened because the bank did not communicate to the employees about CRM implementation programme. It seems to them that CRM is software oriented rather than human oriented.

ENTREPRENEURS CONCENTRATE ON CUSTOMER FEEDBACK

I presented a paper on 'Challenges of CRM' at a two day national seminar conducted at Mangalore for which I was invited for presentation. I was travelling from Bangalore to Mangalore for the presentation of the paper. During the journey, I met an employee working in SAP Company. I did not reveal about my thesis on CRM to him and as a layman I started putting many questions about it. Some of the main points which I discussed for two hours are (1) SAP, at present does not have any customers in India. (2) The attrition rate is as high as any in other software industry. (3) SAP employees think that it is more a software than human ware. (4) No Human Resource element is discussed in development or implementing the CRM packages. (5) SAP does not have any relationship building strategies with their employees. (6) CRM is more information sharing and building techniques. (7) SAP does not practise CRM strategy with their customers. But they do the same for others.

I shared my experience with the audience during my presentation which was followed by the college students on the specific topic "CRM implementation in ICICI Bank – A case study." In their presentation, they stressed that there was lot of difference in customer satisfaction levels among the customers. I asked them, "It is good you had a lot of data from the service provider, but did you collect any data from the customers? The answer was as expected; they did not meet the customers. For the successful implementation of CRM, the customer feedback is the key element.

I do not want to come to any conclusion about bank's service by taking one or two instances. But I want to highlight that ***each customer counts in the company life cycle***. Most importantly, involvement of employees in the CRM implementation is a must to every organisation. With out involvement of people and commitment, no organisation can survive however big it might be.

ENTREPRENEURS ARE AWARE OF THE IMPORTANCE OF CUSTOMERS

Even though customer feedback is important, how many companies collect the feedback? And if they do collect, how many of them have a standard format for it and how frequently do they collect it. These are the big questions to be answered. And the next question is how to collect the true feelings of the customers. All the companies shall keep in mind the following facts. According to one survey, only 16% of the satisfied customers will come for next purchase. Only 40 –50 % of the delighted customers will come for the next purchase. There should be a beginning for collection of feedback. Entrepreneurs concentrate on customer feedback. In case of a small company collecting the customer feedback is not a problem. But how to collect the customer feedback when the company is large? It is simple, do the Pareto analysis (A,B,C analysis) and collect the customer feedback. Collection of customer feedback is a must. ***The journey of thousand miles begins with a small step. Entrepreneurs are aware that happy customers make the organization successful.***

The success of CRM depends more on 'humanware' than 'software'. If the company retains the employees, employees in turn will retain the customers. If a company builds the relationship with the employees by retention who in turn build relationship with the customers. If a long-term relationship is built, all the employees work towards a common goal (i.e., relationship with customers). They work as a magnet as all the atoms are unidirected compared to an iron piece. As we realize the importance of relationship, it is the right time to recollect the quotation **"service begins at home"**.

ENTREPRENEURS ARE AWARE OF *THE POWER OF ONE!*

HOW MUCH A COMPANY LOSES BY ONE CUSTOMER:

Let us assume hypothetically a business which has a revenue of Rs.10 million a year from 2,500 customers. Assuming cost of sales is 66% of revenue, or Rs.6.6 million.

Take the total number of customers and multiply it by 25% (an estimate for this example) to get the number of dissatisfied customers. Multiply that result by 70%, an estimate of the number of dissatisfied customers who will switch to a competitor. Divide total annual revenues by the number of customers to get the average revenue of one customer. Multiply this by the number of customers who have switched over, to get the cost of losing your customers.

Next, calculate the foregone (lost) opportunity revenue by assuming each dissatisfied customer will tell 10 people. Assume that 2% of these will buy elsewhere. Multiply this number by the average revenue per customer to get the potential lost revenue.

To determine customer acquisition and replacement costs, multiply total annual revenue by 66%, and divide that by the total number of customers to replacement cost per customer. Multiply this result by five to get your replacement cost per customer. (since it costs five times as much effort, time, and money to attract a new customer than it does to keep an existing customer)

Now, add up all the results to get the total cost of poor service. Multiply that figure by 10 to determine the costs of poor service over a 10 year period, considered to be the customer's lifetime for doing business with the firm.

No business of any size can afford to lose and acquire customers continuously. These results should motivate the firm to improve the customer service programs so that they focus on *long-term customer retention.* The above calculations are shown below.

THE COST OF POOR SERVICE

Lost Customer Revenue

A. Annual revenue Rs.10, 000,000

B. Total number of customers 2,500

C. Percentage of dissatisfied customers x 0.25

D. Number of dissatisfied customers (C x B) = 625

E. Percentage of dissatisfied customers who are likely to switch x 0.70

F. Number of dissatisfied customers who will switch

= 437.50

G. Average revenue per customer (A / B) Rs. 4,000

H. Revenue lost through poor service (F x G) **Rs. 1,750,000**

Lost Opportunity Revenue

I. Number of other people dissatisfied customers tell (F x 10) = 4,375

J. Number of potential customers who buy elsewhere due to negative word of mouth (Assume one in 50 will tell, therefore I x 0.02) 87.5

K. Potential lost revenue (J x G) **Rs. (350,000)**

Customer Replacement Cost

L. Customer Acquisition costs (66% x A) Rs. 6,600,000

M. Average cost per customer (L / B) Rs. 2,640

N. Replacement cost for lost customers (M x 5) **Rs. 13,200**

Total Costs

O. Total Annual cost (H + K + N) Rs. (2,133,200)

P. Total cost over customer's lifetime of doing business for 10 years (O x 10) **Rs. (21,132,000)**

In this frightening example, the company will lose more than Rs. 2 million a year due to poor service and lower customer retention. Now, a company which does the above calculation and sees the results will probably be awakened to improve customer service and make customer retention efforts.

"Customer service is governed by the rule of 10s. It costs 10,000 to get a new customer; it takes only 10 seconds to lose one, and 10 years to get over it or for the problem to be resolved. We must work to keep our customers."

After knowing how much we lose by the loss of a single customer, it is the right time to know why customers stop doing business with a company.

Customers stop doing business because

- 1% die.
- 3% move away.
- 5% seek alternative or develop other business relationship.
- 9% begin doing business with the competitor.
- 14% are dissatisfied with the product or service.
- 68% are upset with the treatment they have received.

If one looks at these percentages, a company actually has control over 96% of the reasons why customers stop doing business with them. Entrepreneurs must concentrate on this. For example, IBM company mission statement is "Customer satisfaction" and values of the company are defined in terms of customer benefits.

ENTREPRENEURS ARE GOOD MOTIVATORS

"In motivation people, you have got to engage their minds and their HEARTS. I motive people, I hope, by example — and perhaps by excitement by having productive ideas to make others feel INVOLVED."

— Rupert Murdoch.

Entrepreneur should be able to motivate other people. There is no limit to the power of motivation.

This is the example shared by one of my friends. It is from history (Future is uncertain; unluckily in India history is also uncertain because history changes whenever there is change in the ruling government). In

Mahabharata, after the war had concluded between Pandavas and Kouravas the entire battlefield was filled with dead bodies. Gandhari lost all her sons. She was not able to control her sorrow. She wept for many days in the battlefield. After some days, she felt hungry, but nothing was available there. She saw a mango tree near by with only one fruit on it. She went and tried to pick up the mango from the tree but it was too high. She looked for a lengthy stick but could not find it. Her hunger increased. Then she pulled all the dead bodies of her sons and piled them up. Standing on the dead bodies, she could pluck the mango. She plucked the mango and satisfied her hunger.

Man will do any thing to satisfy hunger. If an entrepreneur properly uses motivation and identify the needs of his employees and satisfy them, he can get extraordinary things from ordinary people.

ENTREPRENEURS CONCENTRATE ON PROCESS

"Never tell people how to do things. Tell them what do and they will be surprised with their ingenuity."

— George Patton

A College of Engineering conducted a national management fest. On the first day evening, we had a panel discussion chaired by eminent personalities from the industry. After the presentation, the panel was open to the audience. One of my colleagues asked, "Is it better to be a big fish in big pond or small fish in a big pond?" Please read it carefully it is not "big fish in small pond and small fish in big pond?". There was a lot of discussion on this question. But I strongly believe that as long as you know swimming it does not matter whether you are a big fish or small fish in a big pond. One should not work for the results but work for the organisation.

ENTREPRENEURS PROTECT THEIR STOKEHOLDER'S INTERESTS

Longterm benefit ::THE DILEMMA OF THE DIRECTOR

Spinning Mills Limited, popularly known as 'SUPER A' and 'SUPER B' the two sister concerns of the same group which are strategically located in a backward district of AP. The workforce always exchanged their views and policy matters amongst themselves on a daily basis as they are located nearby.

Mr. Dhanush took over as the Managing Director of the company in 1993 when the company had 25 crore rupees turnover and had a 100 workforce in SUPER A. He was assisted by the functional manager. Mr.Teja (H. R. Manager) was with the company for a long period of time and wanted to maintain good relations with the workforce. Mr. Teja was so effective that the company had only one Trade Union, with cordial relations with the management. Mr. Teja strongly believes in Theory Y, even through majority of the workforce is not highly educated.

Mr. Raja, Production Manager was basically a task master. He does not believe in maintaining good relations. As majority of the workforce is not educated, he believes in the 'carrot and stick ' policy.

Mr. Pramod Mahajan, Marketing Manager was with the company for the past five years. As the company had few good customers in the market, he used to concentrate on other functions of marketing other than selling. He strongly believes in maintaining good relations with the customers.

Mr. Jaswanth, Financial Manager was with the company for the past two years.

Mr. Dhanush, had to deal with the above four personalities and integrate their efforts for the success of the organisation. The company used to give many benefits to the employees other than what was required by the statutory guidelines. Company used to provide good financial and non financial incentives regularly. The company used to pay 30% bonus regularly.

In the global era, every company has to face competition. With LPG, the performance of the company is also affected. The profit of the company started coming down. Mr. Dhanush after seeing the financial performance of the company, he decided to reduce the percentage of bonus from 30 to 10. All the functional managers accepted his decision. The same news spread among all the employees. All the employees were frustrated because they were accustomed to receiving 30% bonus until then.

The management of the company tried to reduce the frustration among the employees by explaining the reasons for reduction in bonus percentage. And also, they promised that if the company gets good profits in the near future, they would increase the bonus to original 30%. Somehow, the employees were not convinced.

One day, the trade union to the management which came as a shock to the management. The Management was not able to digest the same because they had very good relations with the employees for a long time.

The Management called trade union leaders for negotiations. In the process, the trade union was ready to accept 20% Bonus, while management was ready to give 14% bonus. But, both did not come to an agreement. Talks failed. Trade Union was ready to go on strike. Management called them once again for negotiations. Management had slightly increased their percentage to 15 and Trade Union was ready to accept 18%. Again negotiations were in a dead lock. Trade Union met the Local Officer, but Local labour Officer said if the percentage of bonus is less than 8.33% (norm), only then he will come into the picture.

The deadline of the notice approached. Both the parties wanted to take one more chance through negotiation. They assembled for final negotiations. Trade Union was ready to accept a bonus of 17% and

Management was ready to give 16%. Talks failed. Trade Union decided to go ahead with strike. It went on for a month. Even management did not want to compromise. The families of the employees were affected, but they did not want to compromise. At the same time, the company was facing pressure from the customers. Management knew that crores of rupees were locked up. But, still they did not want to compromise.

Financial Manager came up with the calculations. The cost of 1% extra bonus. (Approximately it was around Rs. 5 00 000), the amount of loss they were making by stopping production for one month was Rs. 20, 00 000). The net loss for the company would be Rs.15 00 000 per month. So he wanted to settle the issue by paying 1% extra bonus.

Human Resource Manager was not ready to accept this. His argument was that "it is not the question of the numbers, but it is the question of strength of the management. A compromise will encourage the trade union to go for a strike for every small issue. So let the strike continue."

Production Manager was worried that he may not able to produce the goods in time and crores of investment on machinery is going to be a waste.

Marketing Manager was worried about the customers and if the strike continues for one more month, he may lose some of the orders.

Mr. Dhanush, Managing Director listened to all the views of his team members. He had to take a decision depending on the above facts.

If you were in the position of Mr.Dhanush what would be your action plan?

ENTREPRENEURS ARE OPPORTUNITY SEEKERS

All of you might have come across the success story of *Wrigley* brand chewing gum. The owner of the company first used to sell soda and along with the soda he used to offer detergent free of cost. After a period of time, he observed that customers are more interested in his detergent rather than soda. He stopped producing soda and started selling detergent. To promote this product along with the detergent, he used to offer chewing gum. To his surprise, he found that customers were more interested in chewing gum. He stopped producing detergent and started producing chewing gum. That is how the successful brand Wrigley chewing gum has evolved. He continuously explored opportunities which were there with the customers.

Let us know the full story about it. Even in Small Things, "Quality is Important". William Wrigley Jr. came to Chicago from Philadelphia in the spring of 1891. He was 29 years old, had $32 in his pocket and unlimited enthusiasm and energy. He also had great talent as a salesman.

His father was a soap manufacturer, and at the start of his new business in Chicago, Mr. Wrigley sold Wrigley's Scouring Soap. As an extra incentive to merchants, Mr. Wrigley offered premiums. He knew his customers would be more likely to carry Wrigley's soap if they received a little of "something for nothing." One of these premiums was baking powder. When baking powder proved to be more popular than soap, he switched to the baking powder business.

Then one day in 1892, Mr. Wrigley got the idea of offering two packages of chewing gum with each can of baking powder. The offer was a big success. Once again the premium - chewing gum - seemed more promising than the product it was supposed to promote.

At that time, there were at least a dozen chewing gum companies in the United States, but the industry was relatively undeveloped. Mr. Wrigley decided that chewing gum was the product with potential he had been looking for, so he began marketing it under his own name. His first two brands were Lotta and Vassar. Juicy Fruit gum came next in 1893, and Wrigley's Spearmint was introduced later that same year.

Getting a foothold in the chewing gum business was not easy. Several times, the young company was on the verge of going under, but hard work overcame the difficulties, and the business forged ahead.

In the very early days, William Wrigley Jr. personally did much of the selling to the trade. He had a gift for seeing his customers' point of view and accommodating himself to their needs. As the company grew, Mr. Wrigley showed an unusual knack for inspiring enthusiasm in the people who worked with him.

Mr. Wrigley was also one of the pioneers in the use of advertising to promote the sale of branded merchandise. He saw that consumer acceptance of Wrigley's gum could be built faster by telling people about the benefits of the product through newspaper and magazine ads, outdoor posters and other forms of advertising. Then, as more and more consumers began to ask for and buy Wrigley's chewing gum in the stores, the storekeeper would naturally want to keep sufficient stock of Wrigley brands on hand.

As the company continued to grow, it steadfastly applied this basic principle: "Even in a little thing like a stick of gum, quality is important."

ENTREPRENEURS ARE VISIONARIES

"Where there is no vision, the people perish."

In the words of Ketan Sampat (President, Intel India) "He (Andry Grove) said different things at different times, and time and again the unfolding events have proved him right."

In the early nineties, Grove spoke about the PC being the dominant computing device, and that the number of PCs would be in the range of 100 million by the turn of the century. It happened. He spoke about Intel being the dominant architecture in PC, and it happened as well. In the late nineties, he started talking about a billion connected computers that happened too — there were more than one billion connected machines. "His genius is in being able to paint a compelling picture not just for Intel but the entire industry," says Ketan Sampat.

One more successful visionary is Bill Gates. Bill Gates, who made an enormous impact on software industry and created a lot of wealth was able to visualize the PAPERLESS OFFICE two decades ago. Now, we are marching towards it.

Without a clear vision, we do not know where we are going. Entrepreneurs have to be good visionaries.

COMMITTED TOWARDS QUALITY

"The very essence of leadership is its purpose. And the purpose of leadership is to accomplish a task that is what leadership does and what it does is more important than what it is or how it works."

— Colonel Dandrigde M.Malone

One important feature in Total quality management is top management commitment in addition to the customer satisfaction. Unless top management is committed towards quality, quality cannot be achieved in the organisation. The quality of the organisation is the quality of the products/services. After highlighting this point, I used to give a small case study to the student to what extent they understood the concept. The case study is as follows.

A company decided to implement TQM in the organisation. A customer placed an order for 50,000 units of a product and he also mentioned that he will allow 5000 defects in that. But, he wanted it immediately

When the entrepreneur looked into the stock, there were 45,000 good quality products and also 5000 defective products. If you were to be the entrepreneur, how many items would you supply? Many students answered that they would supply 45000 units of quality items and also 5000 units of defective units. The answer to the above question would be — supply 45000 quality units from our stock and buy 5000 quality items from the market and deliver to the customer as the customers is in urgency.

ENTREPRENEURS HAVE A PASSION FOR WORKING

"Genius is one percent inspiration and ninety nine per-cent perspiration."

— Thomos Alva Edison

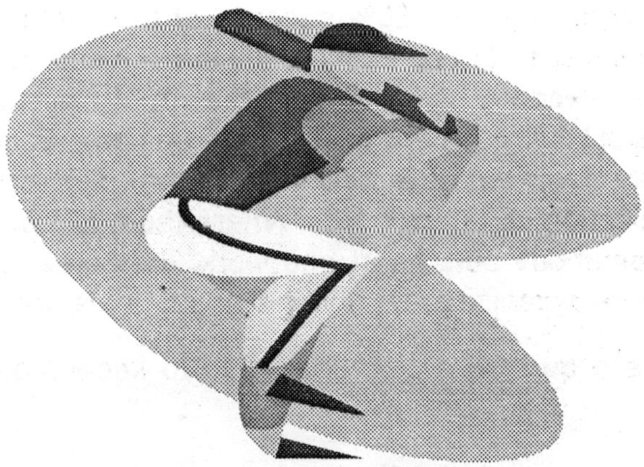

Recently, I was going through the book "The Present" by Spencer Johnson (The author of 'Who moved my Cheese'), which mentioned "be present whatever the job you are doing?" We watch one full day cricket match from morning to evening but we do not feel the strain. Why? Because we love watching cricket match and enjoy the same. Similarly, if we love our job we will enjoy the job.

One best example about a person who works with passion is Mr.Billy Bowden. A cricket umpire has to keep standing from morning to evening, i.e., throughout the match period. You might have seen so many umpires doing the job seriously. But, if you have observed Mr. Billy Bowden from New Zealand, you will notice he does his job with entire body. Sometimes, he will be dancing, sometimes moving from one side to another. He enjoys his job because he has built a passion towards it. *Entrepreneurs enjoy their job and live in the present*.

ENTREPRENEURSHIP QUOTIENT

Though the term is new, the concept is old in India because India has the largest number of entrepreneurs in the world, i.e., our farmers. Each one of them has the qualities of entrepreneurs. As it is said earlier, they take risks, not only with the market but also with nature. Agriculture is dependent on the monsoon, which is unpredictable. If you observe their working style, you can understand that they work from the heart, whatever work they are doing. Entrepreneurship quotient deals with that. In an organisation, how many employees put their heart and work for the company? i.e., how many employees think that it is their own company and work for it? The Pareto's law is also applicable in success of the company, i.e., 80% success of the company is due to 20% of the employees. These 20% of the employees put their heart and work for the company. Just imagine growth of the company, if all 100% employees put their heart and work for the company. Entrepreneurship quotient not only deals with the heart (emotions) part, but also deals with skills (application of knowledge). "Where there is a will, there is a way." When somebody puts heart and work, they create a congenial atmosphere where organizational and individual goals are achieved.

Let us have a quiz on entrepreneurship to know more about our entrepreneurs.

1. Name the man who fought with his father frequently and decided to quit the house at least thrice and who revolutionized two wheeler industry and brought fortunes for the company

    (a) Avanish Bajaj

    (b) Rahul Bajaj

    (c) Rajiv Bajaj

    (d) Ravi Bajaj

2. Name the company which floated by the youngest CEO (at the age of 19, became entrepreneur at the age of 14) of the world, a Bangalorian. The company is basically web solution provider

    (a) Subhas Gopinath

    (b) Suraj Gopinath

    (c) Sunil Gopinath

    (d) Suhas Gopinath

3. Name the co-founder who is recently in the news for wrong reasons. (He was arrested because of MMS scandal). The company has changed its name recently from Baazee to eBay India

    (a) Avanish Bajaj

    (b) Arun Bajaj

    (c) Anil Bajaj

    (d) Avnish Ghose

4. Sameer Gehlaut, 31 CEO who made in roads into online stock broking and real estate. Can you name of the company

    (a) Indian online

    (b) Indian Financial Services

    (c) Indiabulls

    (d) India Bulls Financial Services

5. The biggest deal in telecom industry is Essar_BPL communication deal. The man behind this successful deal is Director Vishal Kampani. Name the company

   (a) Morgen & Stanley

   (b) KPMG

   (c) Standard & Poor

   (d) None of the above

6. Name the Managing Director of GO AIR who strongly belives in low cost airlines. Who surprised the airline industry by ordering 50 aircrafts and he is son of well known industrialist Nusli Wadia

   (a) Rajesh Wadia

   (b) Samir Wadia

   (c) Jeh Wadia

   (d) None of these

7. Selling water in India was unthinkable in 1960 and 70s. But someone dreamt it as possible and started selling water in bottles. Can you name the entrepreneur

   (a) Rajiv Chauhan

   (b) Ramesh Chauhan

   (c) Rajesh Wadia

   (d) Rajiv Wadia

8. "People may talk rubbish most of the time. But if you listen carefully, you will hear something you didn't know" — Anil Moolchandani. He is CEO of

   (a) Archies

   (b) Nirma

   (c) Amazon.com

   (d) Indiatimes.com

9. It is known as "white revolution" in the industry. The brand name is "AMUL." The company is located in Anand, Gujarat. The company name is

   (a) GMF

   (b) GCMMF

   (c) GMMF

   (d) None of the above

10. All of you might be aware about Friendship day, Valentine Day. Could you name the date of "Customers day".

    (a) April 1st

    (b) March 1st

    (c) August 30th

    (d) March 15th

ENTREPRENEURS ARE WORKAHOLICS

They have a ***burning desire*** to achieve what they want to achieve. I repeat, it is not a normal ***desire,*** but it is a ***burning desire***. The

difference is that they think and act throughout the day for their goal/ dream.

There is a difference between successful entrepreneurs and unsuccessful entrepreneurs (not failed). The difference is that the successful entrepreneurs successfully infuse their dreams among their employees whereas unsuccessful entrepreneurs are not successful in inculcating their dreams (vision) among their employees. It is right time to recollect the quotation **"leader's success depends on not what happens in the organisation when he is there but what happens when he is not there.**" If the dreams are properly inculcated among the employees, it does not bring any difference in their performance whether you are there or not. That may be the reason why many professionals are talking much about ***'institutionalization of performance'.***

AGE DOES NOT MATTER TO BECOME AN ENTREPRENEUR

Colonel Harland Sanders has become a world-known figure by marketing his "finger lickin' good" Kentucky Fried Chicken. His chicken is now served daily across the United States as well as in more than eighty other countries. It is one of the largest fast food corporations in the world.

The spectacled Colonel Sanders could easily be identified by his clean, white suite, black string tie, and walking cane. A statue of this man can be seen as far away as on Nathan Road in Kowloon, Hong Kong, for one place.

What makes Colonel Sanders' story so amazing, you might ask. One of the most amazing aspects of his life is the fact that when he reached the **age of sixty-five years**, after running a restaurant for several years, Harland Sanders found himself penniless. He retired and received his first social security cheque which was for one hundred and five dollars. And that was just the beginning of his international fame and financial success story...

Harland Sanders was born in the month of September in the year of 1890. He was the oldest child in a family of five. His father toiled in the coal mines of Kentucky until his death, Sanders had just reached the tender age of six years when he had to take care of his younger brother and sister. With his father gone, her left with responsibility of working and supporting the family along with his mother. She started working in a shirt factory. Harland tended to things at home and learned to cook the meals by his mother's teachings. She taught him several dishes, including fried chicken.

Over the next several years, Harland Sanders worked at a variety of jobs. He started out as a farm hand, then moved on to be a streetcar conductor while he was still just a teenager. From there, he was a fireman on the railroad and finally ended up running a service station. Once again, he used his cooking skills that were learned from his mother to provide meals for travellers who stopped at his service station. As his food became more famous, and his food business grew, he moved onto an actual restaurant nearby.

A few years later, in the year of 1935, when Sanders was forty-five years old, then Governor Ruby Laffoon made him a Kentucky Colonel because of his delectable cooking skills.

Progress is not always for the good of everyone, and in the 1950's, Colonel Harland Sanders got the news of the plans for a new highway which was going to be constructed very shortly. The highway could divert the majority of the traffic away from the town and, with the beginning of the highway, Colonel Sanders saw his successful business coming to an end. He closed the restaurant and retired to a social security cheque of one hundred and five dollars a month. When he received his first month's pension, he decided that he wasn't going to sit in a rocking chair and wait for the government cheques. So, he convinced others to invest in his delicious fried chicken recipe, and Kentucky Fried Chicken, the famous 'KFC' was born.

Colonel Harland Sanders finally retired from the business when he was eighty years old, and stricken with illness.

ENTREPRENEURS KNOW HOW TO NAME AND DEFINE THE BUSINESS

Before defining the business, one should understand in which business they are in if someone is in manufacturing of chairs, can you guess in which business he is in ? He is not in the business of supplying of chairs, or he is not in the business of supplying of wooden furniture, but he is in the business of giving customers 'comfort'. We should understand here that nobody sells the product but sells the 'service' irrespective of whether one produce product or service.

What is in a name?

It requires a lot of intelligence in naming the company. To illustrate an entrepreneur who is producing pencils names his company as M/s Mounica pencils company, tomorrow he is not allowed to produce pens. Ultimately, he will not produce pencils, alone but he is producing writing instruments. If he names the company as 'M/s. Mounica writing equipment company', he is allowed to produce all the varieties of writing instruments including pens, ball point/ink pens/white board markers, sketch pens, pen pencils, permanent markers...etc. But keeping the name of the company as 'Mounica communications limited' is too big where stakeholders may not understand completely in which business they are.

Now, let us comeback to our discussion of business definition. According to Dr. Abel a business definition should answer the following questions.

1. Who is the target group of customers?

Suppose an entrepreneur decides to manufacture clothes, who will be his target group? All the people who are in need of the clothes are target group of customers. This will be a general answer. But one should define for this company's clothes who are the target group of customers. For example: either male or female, children/ teens/ old people, Low income group or middle income group or high income group, Domestic or foreign customers, North Indians or South Indians, Sports persons or military men or organizational employees? Definitely, no company can meet all the above customers.

2. What needs are being satisfied for a selected group of customers?

If it is for children, is it school uniforms or regular wear? Is it for protection of the body from the environment or is it for those who want to be fashionable, daily use or occasional use? Is it for day wear or night wear? Is it for attending interviews or attending marriages? Is it for jogging or for official meet?

An entrepreneur should decide his selected group of customers, what needs are to be satisfied and It is not possible for a business to satisfy all the needs of the selected group of customers.

3. How the needs are satisfied?

For the selected group of customers and for the selected group of their needs, how a company is going to satisfy them is the biggest challenge for an entrepreneur. Whether an entrepreneur is going to satisfy the selected needs with the help of woollen cloth, /cotton cloth/ Terri cotton cloths/nylon/polyester or anything else? To produce the goods, whether one is going for automation or mechanization or labour intensive methods or what else? Because it will decide the most important element in the marketing "***competitive advantage***" - What is one's uniqueness when compared to that of the competitors? (If your competitor is able and copies your competitive advantage, it is no more your competitive advantage).

Here are some of the clearly defined business definitions:

For the above mentioned business, target customers: Male aged between 15 and 25 years with income of Rs.2,00,000 per annum residing in urban area in the domestic market.

Needs of the customer: casuals in the evening and not seasonal product (with different colours of standard sizes (ready made) only.

How the needs are satisfied: cotton cloth with 10% mixed to make more shining with prices between Rs. 300-700 per piece with available technology in the plant (not fully automated).

One need not restrict strictly to the above while doing the business. But one can go for a product line extension or diversification. But the purpose of defining business is to know from where to start and from where we started. The clarity of business definition will make marketing easy. It is rightly said that ***business starts with the customers and ends with the customers.***

Entrepreneurs Take Calculated Risk

The basic problem of the entrepreneurs is they fail to calculate the risk: One should not get confused with the term risk, certainty and uncertainty. In simple terms, risk can be defined as variability of inflows or outflows. For example, you have Rs.1000 and you deposit in a bank, it will give 6% interest on the amount irrespective of economic conditions of the nation. You are sure of getting 6% return. It is an example for certainty. If you buy shares for the same amount, your returns depend on the company's performance. The Company may get 100 crore rupees of profit, but payment of dividend is not a must. It depends on the discretion of Board of Directors. Generally, your return may vary from 0 % to 50%. This is an example for risk where your returns vary with in a known range. If you invest Rs. 1000 in the lotteries/horse races how much will be your return? You may get a very big amount or you may lose your principle also. It is an example for uncertainty where your returns may be from 100% to 3000%.) Coming back to our discussion, entrepreneurs fail to calculate the amount of risk they take by not considering the time value of money.

Suppose, there are two alternatives like whether you spend 300 rupees for 10 years or pay 4000 immediately and pay 120 for the next nine years. Generally, you will go with the first option rather than second one. Because procuring Rs. 4000 is a problem. Do you accept his decision or which alternative will you choose?

Here is an interesting calculation to know the time value of money. Suppose you pay Rs.300 per month for a T.V. dish connection. Do you expect what will be the value of the Rs.300 per month for 30 years? If you pay Rs. 300 monthly, you are paying Rs.3600 annually for 30 years. The value of that amount will be:

3600 X FVIFA 12%,30 = 3600 X 241.33 = Rs. 8,68,788

If you go for DTH connection, you have to deposit Rs. 4000 immediately and Rs.120 per month, after one year onwards. Your total investment in 30 years will be

4000 X FVIF12%,30 + 120 X FVIFA 12%,29

= 4000 X 29.96 + 120 X 230 = 1,19,840 + 3,31,200 = Rs. 4,51,040

In the above frightening example, you save (8,68,788 – 4,51,040 = Rs. 4,17,748) so much by shifting dish connection to DTH connection. (Assuming that Rs.300 per month is constant for the next 30 years, but it may increase to Rs.1000 by the end of 30 years and at the same time DTH Rs. 120 per month may go up by 400 by thirty years.) In the above calculation, we are assuming that compounding is done on annual basis not monthly basis).

Frequently, entrepreneurs borrow money at a high rate of interest and invest in their business. Generally, Banks will not show much interest to lend funds to small scale and medium scale industrialists. It is not uncommon where small scale entrepreneurs borrow funds at Rs. 2 per month per hundred rupees. While borrowing they fail to calculate the time value of money (as shown in the above calculation). Rs. 2 interest per annum means 24% per cent annum. In order to pay back this loan, he has to earn more than 24% say at least 30%, to survive in the business. Otherwise, all his hard earned money as well as his efforts go in vain. By doing little homework on the preparation of Project report and by convincing the Bank officer, the above costs can be avoided.

ENTREPRENEURS DEFINE MISSION OF THE COMPANY

Many a times, entrepreneurs start with one business and end up with an other. This happens because they fail to define the mission of their company. If they have the clarity of the mission of the company, such problem will not arise. Let us examine from an interesting example, how the statement of mission will give the clarity about business and its decision making.

The following example is collected from the book titled "The IBM way".

IBM Company (mission statement: **customer satisfaction**) received a bulk export order. The CEO of the company called for a meeting of all the functional executives including marketing manager on a particular day at 4 p.m. The communication was sent to all the concerned people in advance.

On the scheduled date at 4 p.m., all the concerned executives assembled at the meeting hall except the Marketing manager. The CEO (James Watson) waited for some time for the Marketing manager and then checked with the secretary whether the MM received the message about the meeting and it was confirmed that MM got the message well in advance. At 4.45 p.m., the MM still did not turn up, all the executives were waiting for him and were restless. At 5 p.m., they decided to go ahead with the meeting in the absence of MM (even though the agenda for the meeting was an export order where MM's role was crucial). At 5.05 p.m., suddenly there was knock on the door, the MM was waiting for permission to join the meeting. The CEO did not shout at him, as he was a good listener and wanted to know the reasons for the delay. The MM said, "I am sorry, late for being the meeting. At 1.30 p.m., there was a call from a customer. The customer made a complaint and I thought, I could attend it first and then attend the meeting at 4.00 p.m., but when I attended to it the complaint was could not be resolved early.. I did remember that the meeting was scheduled at 4.00 p.m. Then there was a dilemma in my mind whether to complete the customer work or to attend the meeting. Then I looked into the mission statement of the company, which says **'customer satisfaction'** and then I decided to complete the task and attend the meeting. This is why I am late to the meeting." The CEO appreciated the MM for his customer commitment.

"If you do build a great experience, customers tell each other about that. Word of mouth is very powerful."

— Jeff Bezos

Entrepreneurs should be able to define the mission and communicate the same to their employees properly.

Next time, when you meet the working executives of any company you ask about their company mission statement. Let us see how many of them will be able to recollect their company's mission statement. In India , most of the employees are not aware of their company's mission statement, and those who are aware of it, will not understand it, and those who understand are not interested to implement it, and those who are interested to implement fail to implement because others including superiors will not allow them to do so for the reasons mentioned above.

Entrepreneurs fail to update the changes in customer tastes and preferences, technology, competition, rules and regulations of the market. The strategies, which worked in the past, need not necessarily work at present and in future. Each business situation is different, each day is different, each customer is different and each product is different. To meet the changes, entrepreneurs must update their skills. How many entrepreneurs regularly attend training programs? How many entrepreneurs think that they need training? Training is a must irrespective of irrepresentive of whether one is entrepreneur/ intrapreneur.

ENTREPRENEURS KNOW HOW TO APPLY KNOWLEDGE

A person who thinks he knows everything has the most to learn. There was a Pundit who mastered Geeta and many such scriptures . He was recognized as renowned scholar among the pundits. One day, he was going to a village where he had to travel in a boat. While traveling in a boat, he started conversing with the boat man. Pundit asked "have you studied Geeta? The boatman replied "no master". Pundit said "Half of your life has wasted." Then pundit asked, "have you studied Mahabharata? The boatman replied, "No master." Then Pundit told, "Your remaining part of the life is also wasted." Then Pundit started how tough to read these books and how knowledgeable he was. Then, it started raining heavily. The boatman asked Pundit "do you know how to swim." Then Pundit said "No". Then, boatman said, "It is raining heavily, boating is practically not possible. Even though I haven't studied Geeta and Mahabharata, I know swimming. I am leaving you in the boat and swim by myself for safety." **Knowledge becomes sense only when it is applied properly**. Knowing is not doing, doing is only doing. Knowledge may become nonsense when it can not be used properly. Knowing is not enough for a door he just jumped into the water.

❐ ❐ ❐

CHAPTER 3

Entrepreneurship and Innovation

Innovate or Perish

— A. GROVE

Entrepreneurship and innovation go hand in hand. The starting point of entrepreneurship is a new idea which comes from an innovation.

MARKET INNOVATIONS

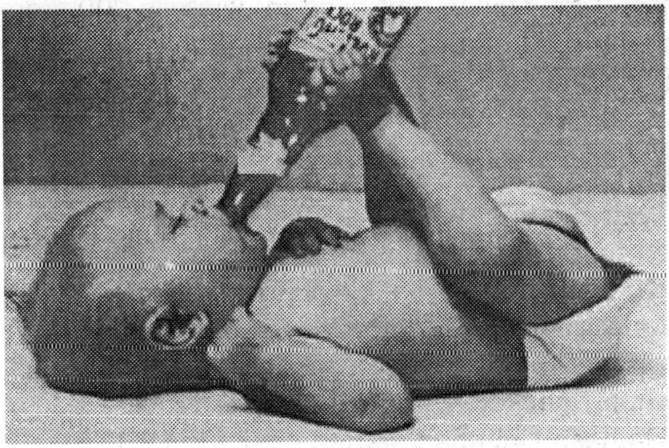

Market identification is like appreciation of beauty. Beauty exists everywhere, but you have to see in the right perspective The following examples justify this. If you ask anybody, "Who are the target customers for chocolates?". Many would say it is children. But, today chocolates are sold more to youth and elders. Companies instead of competing with the available cake .they increased the size of the cake (market)

itself. They start advertising how chocolates can be enjoyed by youth. Today, chocolate boxes are promoted as gift packet also.

One of the sales executives of a shoe manufacturing company was sent to identify the potential market in a backward island. He observed that none wore footwear as there were civilization was a primitive one.(Most of them were illiterates and depended on nearby forests for livehood). He communicated to the company that there is no demand in that island as nobody needs footwear. The company sent its Vice President (Marketing) to the same island; his communication was that "There is a lot of demand here for footwear as nobody uses them. As many of the people are unaware of importance of footwear, we have to educate the locals about footwear. In this context, we have to take the tribal leader into confidence. Though they cannot pay money, but they can trade sweet apple (which are available can plenty). Company can export these apples and can earn 10 million rupees annually."

Here, the Vice President of the company viewed from, an entrepreneurial angle and was able to identify the market.

The market for human hair used for wigs, is 200 crores of rupees per year nearly. One company collects all the hair from the Tirupati Tirumala Devasthanam and exports and earns crores of rupees in profit.

Ramesh Chouhan had shown the way how to sell water in rural India. Yes, you are right we are talking about the Bisleri brand bottled water. When he decided to enter rural market (where selling of water was very difficult), he got an innovative idea. He started supplying bottled water to marriages/ functions in rural area free of cost. After supplying four to five marriages/ functions in the rural area, it became a custom to supply packed water in marriages/functions. Once it became a custom, Ramesh Chouhan started charging for it.

Markets can not only to be identified, but also can be created.

PRODUCT INNOVATIONS

Needs and wants are satisfied with the help of products and services. Identifying the right product/service is a biggest challenge. The 3M Company has 6000 products in its product line. Many of these products have not come from the R & D, but are suggestions of their employees. Entrepreneurs should listen to the suggestions of employees, suppliers, customers and general public and take the right decision in the introduction of a new product.

PROCESS INNOVATIONS

Dell Company was the first one that thought of selling computers directly to the customers without distribution network, which is a normal part of process and achieved a great success. Today, we hear about network marketing which is a part of the process improvement.

Entrepreneurs strongly believe and practice that what they are doing today can be continuously improved further. (In Japanese language, we call it as *Kaizen*).

When enquired on retaining people the corporate world uses knowledge and people management as parameters. The weightage associated is 35% for knowledge and 65% for people management. Even if one is selected by wrong means, he may not sustain in today's corporate world.

When we look at the corporate world, they select the candidates on the basis of knowledge (15%) and attitude (85%). The malpractices may have small impact on knowledge but not major on attitude.

All the IIMs professors might have taught in their classes that every problem is an opportunity. Management guru, the role of management is to convert each problem into an opportunity.

Just go through the following examples.

- A heart surgery in Bangalore under specialist care costs Rs. 1,00,000. Narayana Hrudalaya has shown the way. Rs.5,00,000 and above are charged elsewhere.
- An eye surgery by an expert costs only Rs.10,000. Arabindo Hospitals have made it possible in Chennai. It is remunerative enough for the surgeons as they perform 3 to 4 operations per day; otherwise they would perform only 3 in an average week.
- A big specialty hospital in a drought prone remote place in Mahaboob Nagar in Andhra Pradesh, where many people are below the poverty line, Apollo hospital has shown the way, by charging the patients one Rupee per day as their fee, which actually is towards UTI as insurance. In turn, UTI will reimburse the medical bill to Apollo.
- Television sets costed Rs.16,000 five years ago, but now for just Rs.12,000 and you get even better sets.

All the above is possible with the help of **PROCESS IMPOVEMENT**.

Process Certification

International Organisation for Standardization (ISO) gives the certification on Process standardization. Did all of us know that ISO should not be pronounced as I. S. O.? but *ISO* meaning similar. (like isobars, isoquants). ISO is different from our ISI mark. ISI mark is given by BIS (Bureau of Indian Standards) when a product has a predefined and assured quality. It is surprising to know that ISO is globally accepted, but not ISI. Because, ISO is given for **PROCESS** standardization and ISI is given for product standardization. (For exporters, ISO certification is mandatory).

One important approach for **process improvement** is Value Engineering or Value analysis. Value analysis aims at a systematic identification and elimination of unnecessary costs, resulting in the increased use of alternative, less expensive material, cheaper designs, economic methods of manufacturing (any operation) etc. to provide the same performance, quality and efficiency and reducing overall unit costs thus consequently earn greater profits. For example, a stainless steel part can be replaced by fiber-glass part and thus save costs. More specifically, Value analysis is " the study of the relationship of design, function and cost of any product, material or service with the object of reducing its cost through modification of design or material specification manufactured by a more efficient process, change in source supply (external or internal), or possible elimination or incorporation in a related item."

In simple terms, Value can be defined as

$$\text{Value} = \frac{\text{Function}}{\text{Cost}}$$

Value can be increased by

(1) Reducing the cost for the same function.

(2) Increase in the function for the same cost.

(3) Increasing in function (relatively high) and cost.

VALUE FOR MONEY

"If you don't do it excellently, don't do it at all. Because if it's not excellent, it won't be profitable or fun, and if you are not in business for fun or profit, what the hell are you doing there?"

- Rober Townserd - former Chairman of Avis Corporation.

Nowadays, customers do not think in terms of cost of the product or price of the product. But, they think in terms of 'value for money'. The organizations shall understand the term 'value for money'. Don't confuse 'value' with 'price'. When a consumer buys a product, he does so because that product has a certain value to him. (The cost is up, so you raise your price!) Don't take such an easy way out. It cannot be done. If you raise your price but the value remains the same, you are bound to lose your consumer. So, the organizations are expected to do it excellently.

According to the Union Government, Rs.1, 50,000 crores are spent annually on rural development. Actually, the beneficiaries are denied the benefit, because of process failure. A former Prime Minister states that 'If the government spends 100 rupees, the actual beneficiary will receive only $1/6^{th}$ of it.' It is happening because of Process failure.

One of the comments from one of the alumni of IIM on the drastic reduction on the fees is, "It is like demanding BMW to sell its car at the rate of Maruti car." But, it should be otherwise, if for the same price we can deliver a better value through process improvement.

Now, all IIMs have sufficient reserves with them, now they can concentrate more on research-oriented projects and take this as an opportunity as challenge and earn more and let them show to the country what they are.

"Let us learn from the ***past***

Do things differently at ***present***

Plan for the ***future.***"

Nobody is an exception to the above statement.

SUPPLY CHAIN INNOVATIONS

Is supply chain so important? Yes, when we want to learn management concepts from the rest of world, rest of the world wants to learn from us. Many foreign universities are doing research as to how the concept of six sigma works (actually it is beyond six sigma) from our Dabbawalas.

SUCCESS STORY OF DABBAWALAS

The origin of the Dabbawalas' lunch delivery service dates back to the 1890s during the British raj. At that time, people from various communities migrated to Mumbai for work. As there were no canteens or fast food centers then, if working people did not bring their lunch from home, they had to invariably go hungry. Lunch would not be ready when they left home for work. Besides, different communities had different tastes and preferences which could only be satisfied by a home-cooked meal. Recognizing the need, Mahadeo Havaji Bacche (Mahadeo), a migrant from North Maharashtra, started the lunch delivery service. For his enterprise, Mahadeo recruited youth from the villages neighbouring Mumbai, who were involved in agricultural work. They were willing to come as the income they got from agriculture was not enough to support their large families, and they had no education or skills to get employment in the city. The service started with about 100 Dabbawalas and it cost the client Rs. 2 a month. Gradually, the number of Dabbawalas increased and the service continued even though the founder was no more.

Their mission is to serve their customers — who are mainly office goers — by delivering their lunch boxes at their doorstep on time. They have 5,000 people on their payroll to ensure prompt delivery of lunchboxes within Mumbai; these 'delivery boys' travel by local trains and use bicycles or walk to reach every nook and corner of Mumbai. The lunch boxes are delivered exactly at 12.30 p.m. Later, the empty boxes are collected and taken back to the homes, catering services or hotels before 5 p.m. In fact, the next time you forget to strap on your watch before leaving for office, don't be surprised to find it in the lunch box container brought by the dabbawalla from your home! On an average, every tiffin box changes hands four times and travels 60-70 kilometres in its journey to reach its eventual destination. Each box is differentiated and sorted along the route on the basis of markings on the lid, which gives an indication of the source as well as the destination address.

How the Dabba is Delivered ?

- First Dabbawala picks up the tiffin from home and takes it to the nearest railway station.
- The second Dabbawala sorts out the dabbas at the railway station according to destination and puts them in the luggage carriage.
- The third one travels with the dabbas to the railway stations nearest to the destinations.

- The fourth one picks up dabbas from the railway station and drops them at the offices. The process is reversed in the evenings.

Mumbai has an estimated 5,000 Tiffin carriers — dabbawallas (literal translation — the Box-carriers) delivering about 175,000 lunch boxes every day. The business is certainly old and evolved over a period of time and the efficiency of the process has earned the dabbawallas a six sigma rating from the Forbes magazine.

The Six Sigma quality certification was established by the International Quality Federation in 1986, to judge the quality standards of an organisation. According to an article published in the Forbes magazine in 1998, one mistake for every eight million deliveries constitutes Six Sigma quality standards. The Six sigma rating means that they have a 99.99 % efficiency in delivering the lunch-boxes to the right people. That put them on the list of Six Sigma rated companies, along with multinationals like Motorola and GE. Achieving this rating was no mean feat, considering that the Dabbawalas did not use any technology or paperwork, and that most of them were under graduates. Apart from Forbes, the Dabbawalas have aroused the interest of many other international organizations, media and academia.

Dabbawalla Methodology

- "Error is horror," said Talekar while explaining the operational motto. In the event of a dabbawalla meeting with an accident en route, alternative arrangements are made to deliver the lunch boxes. For example, in a group of 30 dabbawallas catering to an area, five people act as redundant members; it is these members who take the responsibility of delivering the dabbas in case of any untoward happening.

- The dabbawalla must be extremely disciplined. Consuming alcohol while on duty attracts a fine of Rs. 1,000. Unwarranted absenteeism is not tolerated and is treated with a severe fine.

- Every dabbawalla gets a weekly off, usually on Sunday.

- The Gandhi cap serves as a potent symbol of identification in the crowded railway stations. Not wearing the cap attracts a fine of Rs. 25. In fact, Richard Branson, the maverick businessman who is never shy to promote himself and the Virgin brand, donned a Gandhi topi and dhoti (the dabbawallas' signature dress code), during the launch of Virgin's inaugural flights to Mumbai.

- There are no specific selection criteria like age, sex or religion; however, I have never seen a female dabbawalle. The antecedents of the candidates are thoroughly verified and a new employee is taken into the fold on a six-month probation. After that period, the employment is regularized with a salary of Rs.5,000 a month.

Here is a clutch of statistics that reveals the task that the dabbawallas are up to: -

History Started	:	in 1880
Average Literacy Rate	:	8th Grade Schooling
Average Area Coverage	:	60 Km per Tiffin Box
Employee Strength	:	5000
Number of Tiffins	:	2,00,000 Tiffin Boxes, i.e., 4,00,000 transactions every day
Time Taken	:	3 hours (9 a.m. - 12 p.m. delivery of carriers, 2 p.m. - 5 p.m. collection of empty carriers)
Cost of Service	:	Rs. 200/- - Rs. 300/- per month
Turnover	:	Rs. 50 crore per month approximately

FINANCIAL INNOVATIONS

Let us discuss some important financial innovations in Lijjat papad manufacturing unit.

Lijjat Papad Story

Everyone enjoys 'rags to riches' stories and everyone likes tales of stupendous success achieved through sheer determination. The story of Shri Mahila Griha Udyog Lijjat Papad is all that and much more.

Today, **Lijjat** is more than just a household name for 'papad', India's most popular crispy wafer made of Urad dal. Started with a modest loan of Rs. 80, the cooperative now has annual sales exceeding Rs. 301 crore (Rs. 3.1 billion). What's more stunning is its stupendous success and striking simplicity.

And perhaps, that is the most interesting lesson managers can pick up from Shri Mahila Griha Udyog Lijjat Papad. Sticking to its core values for the past forty years, Lijjat has ensured that every process runs smoothly, members earn a comfortable profit, agents get their due share, consumers get the assurance of quality at a reasonable price and society benefits from its donations to various causes.

How has all this been possible? Its story shows how an organisation can infuse Gandhian simplicity in all its activities. Here we look at its distribution cycle.

Every morning, a group of women goes to the Lijjat branch to knead dough, which is then collected by other women who roll it into papads. When these women come in to collect the dough, they also give in the previous day's production, which is tested for quality.

Yet, another team packs the tested papads. Every member gets her share of *vanai* (rolling charge) every day for the work she does and this is possible only because the rest of the system is geared to support it.

Jyoti Naik, President, Shri Mahila Griha Udyog Lijjat Papad explains how the system works.

"The entire cycle starts with a simple recruitment process. Any woman who pledges to adopt the institution's values and who has respect for quality can become a member and co-owner of the organisation."

"In addition to that, those involved in the rolling of the papads also need to have a clean house and space to dry the papads they roll every day. Those who do not have this facility can take up any other responsibilities, like kneading dough or packaging or testing for quality."

"Packed papads are sealed into a box (each box holds 13.6 kg) and the production from each centre is transported to the depot for that area. Mumbai alone has sixteen branches and six depots. Each depot stocks production from the nearby three to four branches — roughly about 400 boxes."

"In some smaller towns or villages, the branch itself serves as the depot. The depots are our storage areas as well as pick up points for distributors."

"Our distributors pick up the quantity papads they require and pay cash on delivery because we pay our *bens* (members are called *bens*, or sisters) every day. Since, we have an estimate of the quantity each distributor takes, we produce accordingly. This ensures that we neither stock inventory nor pay heavily for storage."

"We have about 32 distributors in Mumbai. Each distributor picks up an average of 100 boxes per day from the depot. This is where our job ends. We are not involved in how and where a distributor delivers as long as he stays within the area we have marked for him."

"Generally, each distributor has his three-wheeler and about eight to ten salesmen to deliver to retail outlets within his territory."

"To select a distributor, we first give an advertisement in newspapers for the areas we have marked. Members from our marketing division personally go and check the godown facilities and only on their approval do we appoint distributors."

"A distributor pays us Rs. 150,000 as deposit. We make it clear to them that **they must pay on delivery,** if they want our distributorship. This system is followed all over India and it works well for us."

"When we discover that there is demand in a particular place, we open a new branch, like the recently opened one in Jammu and Kashmir. Whether or not we have a centre in an area, our goods reach there."

"For example, we do not have any centre in Goa, but we have appointed a distributor for that area to ensure that Lijjat papads reach Goa. Our communication with distributors is regular through monthly meetings where we discuss their problems and also the issues that we may have about quality, price, reach, etc."

"We do not have individual door-to-door salesmen or women selling from homes — only the appointed distributor for the area. The same system is followed for other products, but we may have different distributors and depots for different products."

"Exports: Our exports alone account for Rs 10 crore (Rs 100 million). We are not directly involved in exporting, but recognised professional merchant exporters (who also export other food products) place an export order."

"Only on receiving the full advance through a cheque do we begin production. Because all exports are done from Mumbai, the supply also comes from here. Export production is of the same quality as daily production. In fact, we send some of the daily production for export. Again with exporters, our responsibility ends with delivery. They are, both, expected and encouraged to check the goods on collection. After that, where and how they export is their call. At present, 30 per cent to 35 per cent of the production of Lijjat Papad is being exported, mainly to countries like the United States, the United Kingdom, the Middle East, Singapore, Hong Kong and Holland."

"Distributing profits: ***We have accountants in every branch and every centre to maintain daily accounts. Profit (or loss, if any) is shared among all the members of that branch."***

"We have a committee of 21 that decides how the profits are to be distributed. We generally buy gold coins — 5gm or 10 gm, depending on the profit. Everyone gets an equal share of profit, irrespective of who does what work, irrespective of seniority or responsibility. Even a *ben* who has recently joined gets the same share as others who have been with us longer. Each branch calculates its profit and divides it equally among all its members."

"Mumbai has 12,000 members, the rest of Maharashtra has 22,000, and Gujarat has between 5,000 and 7,000 members."

"Decentralization: In two words — decentralization works. We, at Lijjat, have never shied away from sharing power in all our activities. The Sarvodaya philosophy has always been our ideal. All sister members of the institution are the owners. As I mentioned earlier, all profit or loss is shared. Only, we have the authority to decide the manner in which profit or loss should be apportioned among ourselves."

"The committee of 21 members manages the affairs of the institution. There are also Sanchalikas, or supervisors, for each centre to look after the daily affairs of a centre. But, the work of the institution is such that each and every member can take any initiative or any decision. At the same time, each and every member has the veto power. All decisions, major or minor, are based on consensus among members. Any single member's objection can nullify a decision."

"Another important fact about the institution is that no male can become a member and no male employee whether working or honorary or on salary basis has voting rights."

"Other than following this philosophy for our institutional set up, we have try to avoid the usual 'management nightmares.' For instance, production is carried out not in one central location, but in hundreds and thousands of individual homes. The branch system ensures that every activity happens within its own ambit. Testing for quality and packaging are done at every branch."

"Imagine if all the production from all over India were to be gathered at one central office where it would be checked for quality, packed, transported to various depots and distributors, if collection were to be centralised and if distribution of *vanai* and profits too were centralised. Wouldn't it be a logistical nightmare?"

"Our solution is simple. Let the branch be responsible for all activities from production to packaging to collection and distribution of *vanai* and share the profit for its particular geographical region. In following this simple system, we don't need to solve management problems, but can avoid them."

"Certain activities, however, are centralised. For one, all raw materials are purchased in Mumbai and then distributed to the 62 branches to ensure consistent quality of Lijjat Papad. Given the vastness of India, every region produces different quality of urad, rice, spices, et cetera. If procured locally, the final product would never be consistent in quality and Lijjat would have no USP (unique selling proposition) in the market."

"The other centralised process is the grinding of flour. We own two grinding mills, one in Vashi (Navi Mumbai) and one in Nashik (in Maharashtra). Since the raw material is purchased in Mumbai, grinding the flour at our own mills helps reduce costs. Pricing of the products is also done at the head office. Lijjat papads all over India cost Rs. 16.25 a kg. This price factors include the cost of raw materials, transport, taxes, distributors' commission, profit percentage and so on."

Driven by values: Every member who joins in pledges, ". . . . we will make all-round effort to ensure that the *bens* get real fruit of their labour and we will not allow to happen any type of economic loss to the Institution knowingly, unknowingly, directly or indirectly. We are aware that it is one of the very important traditions of our Institution that neither sister-member nor employees take away wrongfully any money or material from the Institution. Those who take away money or materials wrongfully from the Institution are either beggars receiving alms from the *bens* or thugs and robbers extricating bread from a sister's mouth."

"Among others, the chief value that holds the institution firmly is a sense of self-dignity and respect. We discourage any kind of class distinction and do not declare ourselves as an organisation for poor or needy women."

"Our thinking is straight. Ours is a business like any other even if the structure is different. There is no place for feelings of pity, sympathy or charity among members."

"We also do not accept donation or charity of any kind, even if voluntarily offered. I do believe that this has helped the organisation retain independence and brought quick growth. It has given us a clear vision of the path of progress."

"Maintaining proper accounts has always been on our agenda. When we started out, Chhagan Bapa, our mentor had advised us to maintain accounts daily. Even today, every branch closes the account book every day. We do not want to get into monetary hassles because of badly managed accounts."

"There is no place for prejudice on the basis of caste or religion, and democracy in its truest form is encouraged. Following these values ensures that we are run and perceived as a serious business, not a charity organisation. "

Shared Destiny

This cooperative organisation was started by seven women on a terrace of a building in Girgaum in Mumbai. Although only one of those seven survives today, the organisation has not given up on the ideals they started with.

Every member at Lijjat works with a sense of pride in her work. And this pride comes not only from the fact that we produce a good quality product, but also because we have stuck to our core values. That, in turn, has led to a sense of shared destiny in our institution. Every woman earns according to the labour she puts in, but the profits we make as a collective effort are shared equally.

In spirit, we are a nation unto ourselves, almost like a mini-India. We share the same values, are a democratic set up and, like India, have members from every community, every religion, every language within our fold. We work together and dream together for a better tomorrow.

Valuing People

Our beginnings were modest. Seven women with no special skills, but a strong determination to earn dignity as individuals went ahead to make a successful business, doing what they knew best — rolling papads.

They leveraged their basic skill and turned it into a weapon because they believed in themselves and in each other. And that's how we function even today. We believe in each other, in each other's ability and commitment to take the institution towards progress. It is this belief that has been the basis of our business model as well. We understand the family, time and again social pressures women face every day. What we have done is simply to turn these into an advantage and not an excuse. It serves everyone.

Lijjat helps those women who are not encouraged to work outside their homes to contribute to the family income. Our *bens* take dough home and roll them into papads when they are free from their domestic chores.

At the same time, it is not prudent for the organisation to invest in office property for so many members. The perfect fit for both is using the members' homes for the rolling and drying of papads. No additional overhead costs, no investment either. Valuing people and understanding their problems has created for Lijjat a sound and sustainable business model. However, though it would make business sense to adopt modern technology for mass production or use machines for packaging, etc; we haven't done so because it would defeat the very purpose of our existence, which is to provide a source of livelihood and dignity to women through self-employment. In addition, we have one vehicle per branch, which, at fixed times, brings the *bens* and rolled papads to the branch and also drops them back. This is done for all the *bens* — those who mix the dough, do the *vanai* (rolling), testing, packaging, etc.

Delivering quality: We proudly claim 'consistently good quality' to be our USP. From the moment, a new member joins, she is repeatedly told to make quality her mantra. At the training session, *bens* are taught to make the 'perfect' Lijjat papad. And every member has absorbed the concept totally.

It is evident in the fact that even without modern machines, every consumer of Lijjat papad, wherever she is, gets the same consistent quality of papad. How? Because every *ben* rolls the papad to the same specification and every lot of papad goes through testing.

If we find any *ben* becoming careless about quality, we do not tolerate it. We give her a warning, then the option to take up any other work like packaging, testing, etc. and if she still displays a lack of concern for quality, we ask her to leave the organisation.

Out of one kg dough, we must get at least 800 gm (accounting for loss due to moisture, etc), otherwise we cut pay. We get papads for testing from all centres everyday and if we find any deviation from our quality, for example, **if the salt is less or more, etc., we immediately intimate that particular centre to destroy the entire lot, even if amounts to a million rupees worth of production.**

Out of this strong belief in quality delivered at an affordable price comes our act of ignoring competitors. Lots of companies selling papads have come and gone. We don't consider them; we only do our own thing. We do not take into consideration what the competition is doing.

We know that if our quality is good, consumers will buy. Our quality does not differ whether it is for exports or for the local market. There is just one quality: And that's good quality again and again and again.

CULTURAL INNOVATIONS

Let us see how positive Akio is about the employees, what he mentioned in his book 'Made in Japan". An American director of a joint

venture company in Tokyo complained to Akio that he was not able to pin down responsibility for an accident at his company, and he asked Akio why it seemed impossible to discover the name of the culprit, no matter how hard he tried. Akio explained to him that the merit in his company lies precisely in the fact that everybody recognizes responsibility for the accident and that to find one guilty party might destroy the morale of all. Let us see how the culture makes the difference in running the company in the following case study.

SOUTHWEST AIRLINES SUCCESS STORY

Tickets cannot be purchased through common online venues like Orbitz or Travelocity — a minority is booked through travel agents. Most of Southwest's tickets are issued directly by the airline over the phone or online at the company's website which features Web — only fare discounts.

Unlike other major airlines, Southwest allows passengers to change reservations without additional cost. While this provides flexibility to customers, Southwest does not allow same day standby travel on a different flight (usually a free service at other airlines) without upgrading to maximum fare.

Customers are not assigned seats; rather, they are assigned to one of three "boarding groups" depending on their check-in time (earlier check-ins get to board earlier), and are left to choose their own seats on the plane, which helps the airline to board passengers faster. At the May 2006, shareholders meeting, Southwest management announced a study of potentially adopting an assigned-seating system in 2008, as part of a reservations-technology overhaul now under way. As of November 8, 2007, Southwest has implemented an update to their Boarding Procedure in which passengers are now assigned their Boarding letter (A, B or C) along with a number which provides them a specific place in line. The idea behind this is to allow customers not to have to wait in line and spend their time relaxing or catching up on work. They have also introduced Business Select fares, which adds a guaranteed "A" group boarding pass, extra Rapid Rewards credit, and a drink. As a result of the boarding policy, several independent companies have offered automatic check-in services for Southwest. These companies take customer's orders for check-in ahead of the 24 hour mark (when the airline makes a flight available for online check-in) and transmit the necessary data for check-in to Southwest as soon as the airline opens up online check-in for a particular flight. The result of this service is that people using it generally get the first boarding group (known as the "A" boarding group). These early check-in sites include Seat-Sniper.com and CheckinSooner.com. Southwest has not embraced this practice and in fact sued one company (boardfirst.com) in federal district court in Dallas for impermissible commercial use of its website and succeeded in getting the company shut down in October 2007.

Southwest historically allowed three pieces of luggage to be checked in free as opposed to the limit of two on the domestic flights of some other U.S. airlines. Starting January 29, 2008, passengers will be able to check in up to two bags for free. A third bag will be accepted for a $25 charge.

Prior to the 2000s, Southwest served smaller meals than the meals served by full service airlines (now often called "legacy airlines"), with shorter flights receiving single small snacks and soft drinks, and longer flights (with a duration of about 3 hours or more) meriting "Snack Pack"s of prepackaged goods. In the 2000s these meals in a bag typically exceed the food served on full-service airlines like United Airlines or American Airlines. Southwest also offers free in-flight beverages (excluding alcohol). There is no video entertainment. Southwest is known for colourful boarding announcements and crews that burst out in song. The singing is unusual, and is quite popular among customers, but has been noted by some travel critics as being offensive and intrusive.

Southwest maintained excellent customer satisfaction ratings; in 2006, according to the Department of Transportation December year end operating statistics, Southwest ranked number one (lowest number of complaints) of all U.S. airlines for customer complaints, with 0.18 per 100,000 customers enplaned. Southwest Airlines has consistently received the fewest ratio of complaints per passengers boarded of all major U.S. carriers that have been reporting statistics to the Department of Transportation (DOT) since September 1987, which is when the DOT began tracking Customer Satisfaction statistics and publishing its Air Travel Consumer Report.

Rapid Rewards

Southwest's frequent flier program is called Rapid Rewards. Customers receive one credit for each one-way trip (even though the flight may have stopovers). A free ticket, expiring after 11 months, is automatically issued when a member accumulates 16 credits in a 24-month period. Double Rapid Rewards credits used to be awarded for online booking, but this policy was modified at the end of 2003. At that time the bonus was reduced to .5 credit for each segment booked online, (*i.e.*, each round-trip ticket booked online received a total of 3 Rapid Rewards credits). This was discontinued in April 2005. In addition, one-half credit is also earned for using a Southwest partner to book any car rental and/or hotel stay, regardless of whether a Southwest flight is involved or not. This arrangement has won numerous Freddy Awards over the years.

In February 2006, Southwest instituted capacity controls to redeeming its free tickets. This means that the airline limits the seats offered to frequent travellers using free certificates on each flight, whereas previously if there was a seat available, one could use the award, provided the passenger was not flying on one of the five blackout dates.

In early 2006, Southwest expanded its codeshare agreement with ATA Airlines and now allows redemption of award tickets on Hawaii flights at the rate of two awards per round trip flight. Southwest and ATA stress that reward availability to Hawaii will be very limited. Travellers can also earn twice the normal number of credits when they purchase airfare on Hawaii-bound flights.

Advertisements

The company has employed humor in its advertising. Slogans include "Just Plane Smart," "The Somebody Else Up There Who Loves You" and "THE Low Fare Airline". The airline's current slogan is "A Symbol of Freedom". A select history of print and video ads are available on the company website.

Since the 1990s, Southwest has been running a television ad campaign based on the phrase "Wanna get away?" The commercials present comical, embarrassing situations in which people find themselves wanting to "get away." Most ads are accompanied by the sound clip "[ding] You are now free to move about the country"; self-parody of the in-flight announcement that "you are now free to move about the cabin."

Organized Labour

Although Southwest is considered a "low fare" airline, it is heavily unionized when compared to other airlines. The Southwest Airline

Pilots' Association, a union not affiliated with the Air Line Pilots Association, International, represents the airline's pilots. The Aircraft Maintenance Technicians' are represented by the Aircraft Mechanics Fraternal Association (AMFA). Customer Service Agents and Reservation Agents are represented by the International Association of Machinists and Aerospace Workers Union (IAM). Ramp agents and Operations agents are represented by the Transport Workers Union (TWU). Flight Dispatchers are represented by the Southwest Airlines Employee Association (SAEA).

STRUCTURAL INNOVATIONS

One might have observed the recent developments in SBI and other private banks. A customer in the past had to go to different counters for different works like opening account, checking the balance, withdrawing the cash, enquiries etc. But today they have single window scheme where all the transactions can be done in one counter. (Now, a customer can sit and transact in SBI) Such Flat organization structures may be useful in services.

The following are the Thumb rules developed by Prof. Mathew Manimala (Director, Entrepreneurship Development Cell, I.I.M.,Bangalore) for successful Entrepreneurship

- Search for ideas widely, but do at least part of the development.
- Choose project primarily based on one's own interest, capabilities or vision.
- Build one's capabilities, organisations as well as personnel.
- Choose partners for their ideological congruence and complementary capabilities (the same thing is highlighted in the book titles "Big to great".)
- Minimize (initial) investments, test each step and grow incrementally, rely mainly on internal resources.
- Build the company's image through quality of products and customer service.
- Avoid competition rather than fight it.
- Grow by related diversification, especially by vertical integration.

- Change style with the growth of the enterprise.
- Growth relying primarily on internally available resources.
- Build up a formal network of influence around the enterprise.
- Learn from successes, too.

Where there is a will there is a way.

❐ ❐ ❐

CHAPTER 4

Entrepreneur, Entrepreneurship, Enterprise, Entrepreneurs vs Intrapreneurs

"An entrepreneur is the agent who buys factors of production at certain prices in order to combine them into a product with a view to selling it at uncertain prices in future."

— Cantilon

"An entrepreneur is the economic agent who unites all means of production, the labour force of the one and the capital or land of other and who finds in the value of the products which results from their employment, the reconstitution of the entire capital that he utilizes and the value of the wages, the interest and the rent which he pays as well as profit belonging to him."

— J.B.Say.

An entrepreneur is an innovator who introduces something new in the economy. It may be (1) Introduction of a new product, (2) introduction of new methods of production, (3) developing new markets and finding fresh sources of raw materials and making changes in the organization and management.

Peter F Drucker defines entrepreneurs as innovators. They search for changes, respond to them and exploit it as an opportunity. Innovation is the specific tool of entrepreneurs, the means by which they exploit changes as an opportunity for a different business or a different service. It is capable of being presented as a discipline capable of being learned, practiced. Entrepreneurs need to search purposefully for the sources of innovation, the changes and their symptoms that indicate opportunities for successful innovation. They need to know and to apply the principles of successful innovation.

The importance of entrepreneurs to progress cannot be more succinctly expressed than Zin Kin's statement: "No entrepreneur, No development."

"Entrepreneur: An entrepreneur perceives and exploits business opportunities within an existing enterprise. An entrepreneur is an independent businessman whereas an intrapreneur may have to work under another chief executive. An entrepreneur himself raises the required funds whereas an intrapreneur uses the funds raised by his company. An entrepreneur assumes the risks of his business enterprise but an intrapreneur may not be required to bear full risks of his enterprise."

The main points of distinction between an entrepreneur and a manager relate to: Venture (for personal gratification – renders service); risk bearing; Reward; Continuity; Innovation; Status role; Prerequisites.

An entrepreneur always attempts to bring a change in terms of factor proportions, which is called innovation. On the contrary, a manager is concerned only with day to day affairs of a going concern. As an innovator, an entrepreneur establishes a new enterprise and thereby undertakes risks arising from economic uncertainty. But, a manager runs an already established enterprise and thereby undertakes no significant risks. Entrepreneurship involves mobilizing the resources and combining them to initiate changes in production. Management involves combining and coordinating the resources for results.

Entrepreneurs initiate and sustain the process of economic development in the following ways:

- Capital formation;
- Improvement in per capita income;
- Generation of employment;
- Balanced regional development;
- Improvement in living standards;
- Economic independence;
- Backward and forward linkages.

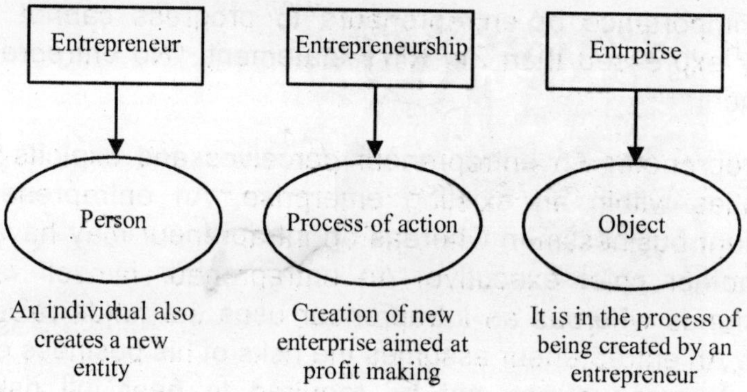

Enterprise may be defined as "an undertaking or adventure involving uncertainty and risk and requiring innovation." It also refers as entity to the ability to think out and start new business. It interacts with other units in the economy, e.g., industry, financial institutions and others. It obtains factors of production from the society and supplies the finished products to the society. Enterprise serves as framework with which decision concerning what to produce, how much to produce, when to produce and how to produce are taken by the owner. Enterprise is an undertaking involving some economic activities, particularly a new though not necessarily an unknown activity.

Different types of enterprise entities:

1. Sole Proprietorship

Sole proprietorship or individual entrepreneurship is a business concern owned and operated by one person. He is a person who carries on business exclusively by and for himself. He alone contributes the capital and skills and solely responsible for the results of the enterprise.

Advantages: simplicity, quick decisions, high secrecy, direct motivation, personal touch, flexibility.

Disadvantages: Limited funds, limited skills, unlimited liability.

2. Partnership Firm

It is an agreement between two or more persons to carry on jointly a lawful business and to share the profits arising from there. Persons who enter into such agreement are known individually as 'partners' and collectively as 'firm'.

Advantages: Ease of formation, larger financial resources, specialization and balanced approach, flexibility of operations, protection of minority interest, capacity for survival, better human and public relations and business secrecy.

Demerits: unlimited liability, limited resources, lack of harmony, lack of continuity, non-transferability of interest.

3. Joint Stock Company

A Joint stock company is an incorporated and voluntary association of individuals with a distinctive name, perpetual succession, limited liability and common seal, and usually having a joint capital divided into transferable shares of a fixed value.

ENTREPRENEURS VS. INTRAPRENEURS

Entrepreneur vs. Intrapreneur

Characteristic	Entrepreneur	Intrapreneur
Behaviour characterized by	Desire for control	Delegation of authority
Management style	One-man show	Management team
Driving force	Creativity-innovation	Status quo
Organisational growth	Rapid response	Strategic planning
Decision-making	Intuitive	Collective information and advice
Definition of aims	In terms of 'vision' terms	In commercial
Attitude towards money	A by-product	Measure of success
Attitude towards risk	Calculated risks	Avoidance of risks
Organisation culture	"Entrepreneurial culture"	"Management culture"

❒ ❒ ❒

CHAPTER 5 Entrepreneurship: How to go about it?

Entrepreneur takes numerous decisions to convert his business idea into a running concern. In setting up his/her enterprise, his/her decision-making process starts with project/product selection. In fact, project selection is the first corner stone laid down in setting up an enterprise. "Well begun is half done."

A project can be defined as a scientifically evolved work plan devised to achieve a specific objective within a specified period of time.

Every project has a starting point, an end point with specific objectives.

Project selection consists of two main steps:

1. Project Identification
2. Project Selection

Project Identification

If you ask any one intending entrepreneur what project he/she will select, the obvious answer would be "a project having a good market." But, the question is how without knowing the product could one determine the market? Whose market will one find out without knowing the item, i.e., product? Idea generation about a few projects provides a way out of above tangle.

Idea Generation

"I am often asked, "Where do you get your ideas?" The short answer is: everywhere. It's like asking, "Where do you find air to breath?" Ideas are all around you."

Project selection process starts with the generation of a product idea. In order to select the most promising project, the entrepreneur needs to generate a few ideas about the possible projects he/she can undertake. The project ideas can be discovered from various — internal and external sources. These may include:

1. Knowledge of potential customer needs.
2. Watching emerging trends in demands for certain products.
3. Scope for producing substitute product.
4. Going through certain professional magazines catering to specific interests like electronics, computers, etc.
5. Success stories of known entrepreneurs or friends or relatives.
6. Making visits to trade fairs and exhibitions displaying new products and services.
7. Meeting with the Government agencies.
8. Ideas given by the knowledgeable persons.
9. Knowledge about the Government policy, concessions and incentives, list of items reserved for exclusive manufacture in small-scale sector, and
10. A new product introduced by the competitor.

Ideas are generated at different places. For someone, it is in the bath room tub, we call him as Archimedes and for someone under a tree we call him Newton and for some one under a banyan tree we call him Buddha, someone thought of flying in the air we call them by John Wright wilber(1867-1912) brothers and for many the general answer is in dreams and mind. The sad story of idea generation is that many ideas die in the mind only.

Success follow ideas or Ideas follow success?

There are successful companies which mainly depend on stakeholders for ideas. If you look into 3M company which is having hnmore than 6000 products in its product line, many products were developed not from R and D but from the ideas of the employees. Secondly, ideas will be generated by observing the environment. It is better to say responding to the environment rather than observing environment.

More ideas are generated when people think differently.

"An idea is salvation by imagination"

— Frnank Lioyd Wright, American Architecty — 1869-1909

One important missile for idea generation is creativity. One should encourage the creativity in the organizations. Creativity is more in childhood rather than at younger age because the more you get experienced the more your mind set is fixed with presumptions which will not allow creative thinking.

IDEAS FROM CRISIS

Ideas might be generated from problems also. The concept of zip is developed by a doctor who got irritated by putting blouse buttons of his wife. The product safety razor blade was developed by a person who had a problem of going to a barber.

Many companies think that they allow the employees to contribute in terms of ideas. But many ideas will die in the initial stages only. Company can do the following survey to know whether they really allow the employees to think and generate ideas.

1. Whether management teaching will help the students to think differently?
2. When will you feel more satisfied?
   (a) When they do whatever you say?
   (b) When they think and do what is good for the organization?
3. Do you think your organization allowed you to think differently?
4. Do you allow your subordinates to think and put forward their own ideas?

5. Could you name some of the new ideas you have accepted from your subordinates?
6. Could you name some of the new ideas you have implemented?

Public do not know what is possible, but an entrepreneur does. So, instead of doing a lot of market research, refine thinking on a product and its use and try to create a market for it by educating and communicating to the market and responding to the environment.

A NEW PRODUCT

"The way to get good ideas is to get lots of ideas and throw the bad ones away."

— Linus Pauling

Here are some of the ideas for products:

Modular Design: is one which combines the two product features: like two in one, (tape recorder and radio), three in one, four in one or all in one, Robust design: an existing product can be made more robust, i.e., to withstand at various working conditions.

Poke a Yoke: (Fool proof) design. Which means that customer friendly usage of the product. Even a fool should not be allowed to do a mistake while using the product. (Example: design of pressure cooker: you can't open the lid before lifting? the weight to release pressure, dissection box, 3 pin plugs, elevators (unless the door is closed it will not move).

Different ideas can be applied in motivation, training, recruitment performance appraisal, sales promotion, production, maintaining value chain ....etc. There is no area in which ideas cannot be implemented. It is rightly quoted by John Kennedy as "***A man may die, nations may rise and fall, but an idea lives on***." Last but not the least, the '*I*'deas generate from " ***I*** ".

PROJECT SELECTION

Project selection starts from where project identification ends. After having some project ideas, these are analyzed in the light of existing economic conditions, the government policy and so on. A tool generally used for this purpose is, what is called in the managerial jargon, SWOT analysis. The intending entrepreneur analyses his/her strengths and weaknesses as well as opportunities/competitive advantages and threats/challenges offered by each of the project ideas. On the basis of this analysis, the most suitable idea is finally selected to convert it into an enterprise.

Project identification is half done in the process of establishing an enterprise. The entrepreneur needs to analyse other related aspects also like raw material, potential market, labour, capital, location, other forms of ownership, etc.

PROJECT FORMULATION

Formulation of project report/business plan is one of the first corner stones to be laid down in setting up an enterprise.

Meaning of Project Report

Project report or business plan is a written statement of what an entrepreneur proposes to take up. It is a kind of guide or course of action what the entrepreneur hopes to achieve in his business and how is he going to achieve it. In other words, project report serves like a kind of big road map to reach the destination determined by the entrepreneur. Thus, a project report can be defined as a well evolved course of action devised to achieve the specified objective within a specified period of time. So to say, it is an operating document.

Contents of a Project Report

1. **General Information:** Information on product profile and product details.
2. **Promoter:** His/her educational qualification, work experience, project related experience.
3. **Location:** Exact location of the project, lease or freehold, locational advantages.
4. **Land and Building:** Land area, construction area, type of construction, cost of construction, detailed plan and estimate along with plant layout.

5. **Plant and Machinery:** Details of machinery required, capacity, suppliers, cost, various alternatives available, cost of miscellaneous assets.
6. **Production Process:** Description of production process, process chart, technical know-how, technology alternatives available, production programme.
7. **Utilities:** Water, power, steam, compressed air requirements, cost estimates, sources of utilities.
8. **Transport and Communication:** Mode, possibility of getting, costs.
9. **Raw Material:** List of raw material required by quality and quantity, sources of procurement, cost of raw material, tie-up arrangements, if any, for procurement of raw material, alternative raw material, if any.
10. **Manpower:** Manpower requirement by skilled and semi-skilled, sources of manpower supply, cost of procurement, requirement for training and its cost.
11. **Products:** Product mix, estimated sales, distribution channels, competition and their capacities, product standard, input-output ratio, product substitute.
12. **Market:** End-users of product, distribution of market as local, national, international trade practices, sales promotion devices, proposed market research.
13. **Requirement of Working Capital:** Working capital required, sources of working capital, need for collateral security, nature and extent of credit facilities offered and available.
14. **Requirement of Funds:** Break-up of project cost in terms of costs of land, building, machinery, miscellaneous assets, preliminary expenses, contingencies and margin money for working capital, arrangements for meeting the cost of setting up of the project.
15. Cost of Production and Profitability of the first ten years
16. Break-Even Analysis
17. Schedule of Implementation

PROJECT IMPLEMENTATION

Last but by no means the least; every entrepreneur should draw an implementation chart or a time-table for his project to ensure the timely completion of all activities involved in setting up an enterprise. Timely implementation is important because if there is a delay, it causes, among other things, a project cost overrun. In India, delay in project implementation has become a common feature. Delay in project implementation jeopardizes the financial viability of the project, on the one hand, and props up (the entrepreneur) to drop the idea to set up an enterprise, on the other. Hence, there is a need to draw up an implementation schedule for the project and then to adhere to it.

SPECIMEN OF A PROJECT REPORT

Project Profile for Manufacturing Unit............................

A. PRODUCT DESCRIPTION

B. PRODUCTION AND GENERAL EVALUATION OF PROSPECTS:

C. MARKET ASPECTS

1. Users:
2. Sales Channels and Methods:
3. Geographical Extent of Market:
4. Competitive Situation:
   (a) Domestic Market
   (b) Export Market
5. Market needed for plant described:

D. PRODUCTION REQUIREMENTS

Salient Features

1. Annual Capacity (One/Two/Three-Shift Operation)
2. Capital Requirements

Land and Buildings on rent (Mention value, of owned)

Equipment, furniture and fittings

Working Capital

3. Total capital which the entrepreneur would need for the whole project provided he uses agencies planned by the Government for financial accommodation as discussed in the book:
   (i) Own
   (ii) Borrowings
4. Expected net profit per annum

E. CAPITAL REQUIREMENTS

1. Fixed assets and working capital

   Land (.......sq. meters) and Building(........sq. meters) on rent at Rs..........per annum

   Equipments:

   (i) Production Equipment (List down in an appendix, giving values, etc., of each machine separately)

   (ii) Other Tools and Equipment

   (iii) Furniture and Fittings

Working Capital

[This would be calculated keeping in view the periods during which capital on an average in various forms, i.e. manufactured goods, semi-manufactured goods, raw material etc., would remain locked up. Often you may calculate it at 3 months requirement level, unless the situation (line of industry) warrants otherwise]

Total

II. Raw Material & Allied Supplies (Annual)

Description	Qty	Rate Rs.	Annual Requirements
1.			
2.			
3.			
4.			
5. Power, Fuel and Water			
6. Maintenance and Allied Supplies			
7. Other Supplies			
		Total	

III. Manpower (Annual)

Description	No.	Rate (Rs.) Per month	Annual Cost (Rs.)
Manager			
Foreman			
Supervisors			
Skilled Workers			
Semi-Skilled Workers			
Unskilled Workers			
Office Staff			
Others			
		Total	

IV. Other Costs (Annual)

(a) Depreciation on equipment, furniture & fittings ....annum

(b) Interest on capital (fixed and working ....per annum on average)

(c) Administrative costs

(d) Sales cost (Including Sales Commission, Advertisement, etc,)

(e) Provision for discount, bad debts and miscellaneous contingencies

(f) Training costs

F. TOTAL ANNUAL COSTS, SALES REVENUE AND NET PROFITS

(a) Annual Costs

(i) Rent for Land and Buildings

(ii) Raw Materials and Allied

(iii) Manpower

(iv) Other Costs Total

(b) Annual Sales Revenue

(c) Expected Annual Net Profit (b-a) say

(d) % Profit on Own Capital

(e) % Profit on Total Annual Sales Turnover

(f) % on Total Investment

While evaluating the project report not only we have to see the figures in the report, but also the spirit behind it. If an entrepreneur is able to communicate his right sprit to the financier, the chances of getting loan will be brightened.

❑ ❑ ❑

CHAPTER 6

Problems of Entrepreneurs: How to Overcome Them?

"In every problem there is an opportunity."

Many entrepreneurs fail due to several barriers and problems. Karl H Vasper has identified the following barriers

- Lack of viable concept
- Lack of market knowledge
- Lack of technical skills
- Lack of seed capital
- Lack of business know-how
- Complacency — lack of motivation

- Time pressures and distractions
- Legal constraints and regulations
- Monopoly and protectionism
- Inhibitions due to patents
- Government policy

Let us discuss some of the above points in detail

"Fail to Market"

There was an interesting punch line for the A & M magazine (now it is not under publication). It was **"Business *is marketing.*"** There are many activities in running a business. All of them are cash outflow activities except customer through which cash inflows are generated. Through marketing, one can create a customer.

Marketing becomes easy when we think from the customer's point of view. Just go through the following idea. We have pain balms available in the market. To ease the way of application, one can think of introduction of pain balm spray. The idea is very good. Recently, one company introduced the pain balm spray. But it failed. Practically speaking, when a spray is applied to the body, it will spread into the adjacent parts of the body and may cause inconvenience or irritation. For example, when one is having headache, if it is sprayed, there is every possibility that it may stretch out to the eyes.

After the successful introduction of two burner stoves, many companies introduced three and four burner stoves, but they failed. Logically, it is correct that if housewife uses all the four burners in a stove she may complete the cooking early. But, the housewife does not want to be projected as an idle woman after completing cooking early. She wants to be projected as always busy person in the home.

It will be surprising to note that the success formula for making Pepsi is sold for mere 500 dollars by a drunkard scientist. The original version of MS DOS, i.e., Quick Dos was sold to Microsoft for $50,000. Many Ayurvedic medicines fail in marketing even though they have good medicinal value.

Rural people work with their heart whatever the job they are doing. Let us see in the following example as to how easily they can sell their product. A woman entered into the railway compartment with a basket of guavas, which were very small in size. I was enthusiastic to know how she could sell the guavas, as the fruits were very small in size. She started offering fruits to the passengers by saying, "Anna (brother) please taste it, you need not buy it, you can think of buying if the fruits are sweet, otherwise you need not buy." within half an hour the fruit basket was empty. Nobody taught her the marketing strategies.

Lack of Technical Skills

"Technical skill is a mastery of complexity, while creativity is a mastery of simplicity."

The CEO of MTR company knows how to cook at least one variety of company's product line. IITs are able to produce more entrepreneurs than Indian Institutes of Management. This might be because of the technical knowledge they have. Technology gives innovations. Innovations lead to entrepreneurship. (Refer to the chapter Entrepreneurship and Innovations).

Lack of Focus

"Concentrate all your thought on work at hand. The sun's rays do not burn until brought to a focus."

There is a well-known anecdote in the Mahabharat: one day during archery practice, Dronacharya pointed out a dummy parrot on a banyan tree, to his students. He then enquired them individually to state what they noticed. Duryodhana replied that he could see the leaves on the large tree, its trunk, branches and also the bird. Most of the students responded similarly. But, Arujuna's words were strikingly different. He said, I see nothing but the eye of the bird." That is why Arjuna became a favorite student of Dronacharya. His entire attention focused on one important spot of the target. This holds the key to successful management.

When entrepreneurs want to do many businesses at a time, they can not concentrate fully on any one of them. Each business to be successful, needs one's full attention. But generally entrepreneurs one inclined towards doing more business because they think theory are safe that way.

Lack of Time Consciousness

A crop will give good yield when fertilizers are applied at the right time. An iron can be bent easily in the required direction when it is hot. God has given exactly 24 hours for the a richest man in the world as well as poorest man in the world. Generally, those who are not time conscioues, they will end up as unsuccessful entrepreneurs.

Lack of Training

"If you wait until you are sure, you will never take off the training wheels."

If you are not updated, you are outdated. Many entrepreneurs start the enterprise with their technical knowledge. With changes in the environment, they are required to get more training. But, entrepreneurs generally do not invest time on training and end up being in trouble.

Lack of Customer Contact

When an enterprise grows, all its efforts are directed towards in administrative activities. Slowly the entrepreneur will lose contact with the customer. Then the decline of the enterprise will start.

Lack of Working Capital

"The working capital reserve will enable us to essentially lend money to ourselves, as opposed to borrowing from outside financial institutions. This will save us considerable time and money."

When an entrepreneur starts a business with limited funds or when he diverts funds to some other use, he has to face acute shortage of working capital. Then, he is forced to borrow the funds at much higher rates of interest (sometimes at 24 % to 30%). Once he borrows at such high rates, he will end up in a debt trap. Whatever the funds generated by an enterprise they should be sufficient to repay the principle and interest.

To make more sales, entrepreneurs supply products on credit. In the process, he requires more working capital as the funds are locked up in credit sales. If few customers become defaulters, then the entrepreneur will be in deep trouble.

HOW TO OVERCOME THE PROBLEMS?

Entrepreneurs should Inculcate Team Spirit Among Employees

"Success for leadership is . . . knowing the great art of leading others without their noticing it."

The fable of tortoise and rabbit is a lesson for all of us. A tortoise and a rabbit planned for a running race.... The Rabbit slept in between thinking that tortoise cannot run faster. I hope all of you have heard the story. Now the rabbit learnt a lesson "*one should not take rest until the goal is achieved*". The next time, again they planned for a running race and this time rabbit won. Third day again, they planned a running race, but this time tortoise decided about the destination to be reached. The rabbit accepted the offer without thinking. To reach the destination, one has to travel half of the distance on the ground and the remaining in the water. Rabbit ran very fast for the first half distance on the ground and accepted the defeat as it did not to know how to swim. the Rabbit learnt one more lesson, "*Do not accept the offer without thinking.*" (Both rabbit and tortoise sat and thought that there was no fun in the game as always one had to lose (it is win –lose or situation game). They thought of another alternative to achieve win-win. This time rabbit carried the tortoise first half distance (on the ground) and tortoise carried the rabbit for the second half distance on the water. Both of them put together reached the destination much earlier than before. Now, they found fun in the game. Similarly, a leader has to plan for the win - win situation and achieve the desired goals with the help of team network.

Should take the Right Decisions at the Right Time

"There are three essentials to leadership: competency, clarity and courage."

Leaders need not posses all the qualities to become successful. Even if one excels few other quantities, will follow. Suppose, one practises a simple quality such as 'punctuality' it will take care of many other related qualities because if one wants to maintain punctuality, he will automatically have many other qualities like attitude, time management, decision-making, etc. Even after passage of several decades, the entire world still remembers Mahatma Gandhi. If one looks into the reason for it, it is because of his qualities. Mahatma Gandhi might have practised qualities like punctuality, honesty, non-violence and commitment with self discipline......

In one of the recent articles in India Today weekly, there were some interesting facts relating to a survey about the best Prime Minister of India. Guess who? It was not Mr. Atalji or Dr. ManMohan or Mr. L.B. Sastry or Mr. Rajiv or Mr.Nehru, but it was Mrs.Indira Gandhi. She got 32% of votes and none of our ex- P.M. got more than 10% of votes. I was thinking about what were the greatest qualities her. (Then, I realized that she was basically an 'aggressive decision- Maker'.

Leadership is not the combination of all identified best qualities. Even if they practise the best three or four, the rest will follow automatically. (the same logic is applicable for entrepreneurs also) The logic behind telling these stories of great people of our country and some events that happened in our country is to in you the great qualities of leaders and their values. But unfortunately, in schools, today children hardly get to know anything about their people which has a strong impact on the child's mind. We hope to see many Mahatma Gandhi, Indira Gandhi and Nehru in future. Will institutions make them like that?

Entrepreneurs shall Love both Enterprise and Employees

"Take care of your employees; employees will take care of your busines".

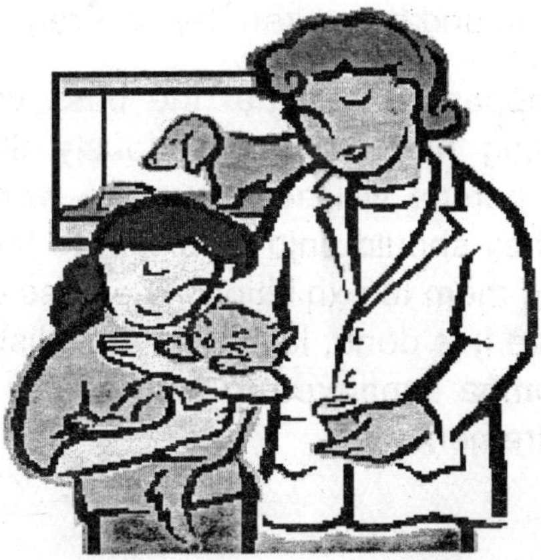

"Too often we underestimate the power of a touch, a smile, a kind word, a listening ear, an honest compliment, or the smallest act of caring, all of which have the potential to turn a life around."

— Leo Buscaglia

Empower your employees, who in turn will empower the customers.

Scientists at the Rocket launching station in Thumba had the habit of working for nearly 12 to 18 hours a day. There were about seventy such scientists working on a project. All the scientists were really frustrated due to the pressure of work and the demands of their boss but everyone was loyal to him and did not think of quitting the job. One day, one scientist came to his boss and told him, "Sir, I have promised my children that I will take them to the exhibition that is going on in our township. So I want to leave office at 5.30 p.m." His boss replied, "O K, You are permitted to leave the office early today." The scientist started working. He continued his work after lunch. As usual, he got involved in to such an extent that he looked at his watch when he felt he was close to completion. The time was 8.30 p.m.

Suddenly, he remembered promise he had made to his children. He looked for his boss, He was not there. Having told him in the morning itself, he closed everything and left for home. Deep within himself, he was feeling guilty for having disappointed his children. When he reached home, children were not there. His wife alone was sitting in the hall and reading magazines. The situation was explosive; any talk would boomerang on him. His wife asked him, "Would you like to have coffee or shall I straight away serve dinner if you are hungry.?"

The man replied, "If you like to have coffee, I too will have but what about Children??? Wife replied — "You don't know — Your manager came at 5 15 p.m and has taken the children to the exhibition."

What had really happened was that the boss who granted him permission was observing him working seriously till 5.00 p.m. He thought to himself, this person will not leave the work, but if he has promised his children, they should enjoy the visit to the exhibition. So, he took the lead in taking them to exhibition. The boss does not have to do it every time. But once it is done, loyalty is established. That is why all the scientists at Thumba continued to work under their boss even though the stress was tremendous.

By the way, can you hazard a guess as to who the boss was?

He was A P J Abdul Kalam. The motto is simple. ***Take care of you employees; employees will take care of your business.***

Should Concentrate on the Right Things

Entrepreneurs should concentrate on the right things.

A group of alumni, highly established in their careers, got together to visit their old University Professor. Conversation soon turned into complaints about stress in work and life. Offering his guests coffee, the Professor went in to the kitchen and returned with a large pot of coffee and an assortment of cups — porcelain, plastic, glass, crystal, some plain looking, some expensive, some exquisite — telling them to help themselves to hot coffee.

When all the students had a cup of coffee in hand, the professor said: Have you noticed, all the nice looking expensive cups were taken up, leaving behind the plain and cheap ones. While it is normal for each of you to want only the best for yourselves, that is the source of your problems and stress. What all of you really wanted was coffee, not the cup, but you consciously went for the best cups and were eyeing each other's cups. Now, if life is coffee, then the jobs, money and position in society are the cups. They are just tools to hold and contain life, but the quality of life doesn't change. Sometimes, by concentrating only on the cup, we fail to enjoy the coffee in it."

So, don't let the cups drive you... enjoy the coffee instead.

Entrepreneurs Should Love their Job

An employee went to a Guruji and asked, "Guruji life had become boring and routine in the job, because of doing the same job every day, dealing with the same people, same complaints, and same problems everyday. But I am not bored in my personal life with the same wife and same children. What might be the reason?" Guruji answered, "Your mother is cooking for you, for so many years, did she get bored any time by doing the repetitive job?" The employee answered: "No". Then Guruji continued "Why did she not get bored?. Because she does not consider it a as work. In a real sense, she is not working but serving. If you also start serve in your job, definitely you will not feel the job as a routine one, rather you would enjoy the job. I wish you enjoy the joy by serving but not working."

Love your job. Your are not working, but you are enjoying it.

Entrepreneurs Should not Look for Perfection

Go through this and write your comment immediately to understand how perception deceives us.

HOUSE

HOUSE WORK

HOUSE WIFE

HOUSE OWNER

HOUSE RENT

What is your comment on the above. Please write your answer before continuing further.

Many of us have the same answer, i.e., the third one spelling is wrong. House is misspellt as HAUSE. In the above, only 20% is wrong. 80% is correct. We always concentrate on negative things rather than positive things. We should have concentrated on positive things and we should have told that four were right in the above. Entrepreneurs should always concentrate on positive things in their organisation.

Entrepreneurs should concentrate on how to get things done and how to make employees responsible

"What we can or cannot do, what we consider possible or

impossible, is rarely a function of our true capability. It is more likely a function of our beliefs about who we are."

— Bertrand Russell 1872-1970, British Philosopher

The biggest challenge for an entrepreneur is getting things done through others and making the employees responsible. An effort is being made to induce responsibility among the employees. The following steps individually or all put together may be helpful to achieve that purpose.

Show by Example through Systems Approach

Entrepreneurs should practise systems approach in solving the problems of the customers. Let us see in the following example what is meant by a systems approach. One of the South East Asian countries found oil reserves in their country. But that country did not have the technology. It called for bids for exploring oil from the ground. Out of all the bids, they finally selected two bids, one was Japanese and the other was American. Japanese quotation was quite high when compared to the American one. But, still the Japanese was selected because in their offer they offered the following services, even though bid was called for exploration of oil; Exploration of oil from ground, Processing of oil, construction of storage facilities, training the local people in the next five years for processes, transportation of oil from place to place and construction of oil pumps. the Japanese firm looked at the problems from the systems point of view and. *When entrepreneurs solve the problems of the customers through the system approach, employees will also practise the same in solving the problems of the customers.*

Should Select the Employees who Fit into the Culture

Long back, at IIM-A, a small company called Western India Products came for campus recruitment. When compared to the remaining companies, it was a small company. Many students did not opt it. But, one brilliant students wanted to take a chance with the company. Only one question was asked at the interview It was, "You have an appointment with one big customer at 10.00 a.m. who makes a lot of difference to the company, being a Marketing executive you want to rush to the customer at any cost by 10.00 a.m. But, by mistake your vehicle enters into one-way road and is stopped by the Traffic Constable. theTraffic constable asks bribe to avoid fine: In that case will you pay the fine or bribe the Traffic constable? You have some money to bribe, but not to pay the fine. Of course, all of you can guess the answer. If the answer were "I will bribe the constable as the time is important for me." You would not have been selected. If your answer was 'I will pay the fine, by calling some friend to come and pay the money, because time is important for me." You would have been selected. The person who was the interviewer was none other than Mr. A. Premji. The company today is known as WIPRO. That is one of the reasons why people always look for attitude rather than only skill in selection process. Mr. Premiji had given lot of importance in the selection of the employees particularly whether the candidate will fit into the culture or not. That may be the reason why the attrition rate is the lowest in the industry.

Here are the findings from a small survey, which was conducted to write this book.

The study is conducted among the employees with an experience of 5 months to 8 years, at junior level to middle level. The findings are as following:

- All the employees opined that they were well received in the organisation.
- But, only 60% of the respondents were satisfied with induction programme and 40% of the respondents were dissatisfied with the induction programme.
- 100% of the respondents opined that the induction programme was necessary.
- 60% of the respondents opined that the induction programme given to them is insufficient.
- For 40% of the respondents, the induction programme is only for 1 to 2 hours and to the remaining it is for 1 to 2 days.
- Only 20% respondents opined that there was resistance from the employees about his joining.
- The following are the important suggestions to make induction more effective.

    1. Give a warm welcome to an employee and give him a brief summary of the company's mission, objectives, goals and information about the company's competitors, rules and regulations.
    2. Arrange an interaction with the entire top management. The management should inform how much an employee is valuable and how each one as is indispensable? Thus, make an employee part of the organisation.
    3. Induction shall be more interactive. Give overall picture (culture) of the organization and with some fun events. The candidate should be clearly told about his role before performing the job. A team of candidates can be given induction programme so that they also get to know each other and team spirit can be developed.

Induction should solve the purpose. There is a feedback at each and every human resource management activity but not in induction. Let the organisations plan for it and then only they will know the problems of new employees and can overcome in future to make the induction programme more effective.

For a successful induction programme, many times small things make a big difference. Definitely, smile is one among them.

"Sometime the smallest of a gesture goes right to the heart...

A smile from a stranger when you are in the of crowd,

An old calling from a distant land just to say ' I miss you'?

The touch of a mother's hand on your forehead when you're unable to sleep,

A message from a friend asking you what was wrong when you thought no one could notice,

And a hand on your shoulder when you feel that the world is against you, sometimes it is the tiniest of things that bring a smile in hard time."

Induction need not be a formal namesake programme but it should be more informal and socialization process.

❑ ❑ ❑

CHAPTER 7

Ethical Practices in Entrepreneurship

Many definitions of ethics in different books help one who wants to practise ethics to choose one, which is favourable to him. What is ethical to one may not be ethical to the other. Here are some of the definitions of ethics.

Ethics = values + knowledge + corporate philosophy

The word refers to principles of behaviour that distinguishes between what is good and bad and right and wrong.

Ethics are defined by Mr. Zen Beuten, "Ethics serve as basis for assessing the "rightness" of potential action."

THE POWER OF ETHICS

By practising ethics, we can attract more and more customers. Oh! not convinced then, go through this real story carefully.

COLT is the brand name of automobile batteries in Bangalore, headed by Mr.Nehruji. As it is a local brand, it has to compete with the national and international brands. It finds a niche in those who look for lower price. Mr. Nehruji, CEO of the company himself shared this story. One day, when he was in the office, he saw a heated conversation going on between his sales executive and a Sardarji. Mr. Nehruji walked in and enquired about the problem. Sardarji in a high pitch said, "I had bought a battery recently and now it is not working properly. The life of my car battery is not over, and wherever I went all the battery manufacturers were telling that was time to replace the battery. But, I am not convinced. I think it can be repaired, need not be replaced " The

CEO himself checked the battery and found that there was no requirement for replacement of battery and it only required a small repair. Then, he asked his sales executive for a second hand battery, so that the Sardarji could leave the defective battery in the workshop for day. Meanwhile, he could use the second hand battery instead. But, his employee said that there was no second hand battery available for temporary replacement, but a new one was available which the Sardarji would have to buy. Then, Mr. Nehruji understood the ulterior motive of the employee, and he searched for a second hand battery and asked the employee to fit it in Sardharji's vehicle. Mr. Nehruji said to Sardarji that "your car battery requires a small repair, I will get it repaired by tomorrow, you go ahead with our second hand battery for one day.Tomorrow you can come and collect your car battery and they will fit it to your car. There is no charge for the second hand battery, and you have to pay for the repair Sardarji felt very happy, and the next day he came and collected his car battery. Mr. Nehruji thought there ended the story. After one week, the vehicles of defense people (who need batteries) started coming to COLT office. Mr. Nehru wondered how so many new customers have started coming for the batteries. When he enquired, he found that the Sardarji who came sometime back was a military commander and recommended COLT batteries to all his friends and relatives. That is ***the power of ethics***. If you behave ethically with **one** customer, he will bring another **ten.**

Thus, by practising ethics we gain more and more.

Everyone shall Practise Ethics at Each and Every Stage

One of my ex-colleagues visited the USA long back. The tax collection system in the USA is different from to India, where tax is paid immediately on any item. There will be two boxes at each counter; one for actual price of the product and the other one for the tax amount in the price. One day, he went along with his friend to a shop to buy bananas. The sales girl at the counter informed them that if they bought one banana, there was no tax and if they bought two bananas at a time, you would have to pay tax on both. Even though, they were in need of two bananas (as they were two), they bought two bananas separately to avoid the tax. The sales girl understood the motive of their deal and sold the two bananas at a time, but paid the tax amount from her pocket (her daily earnings). The customers were shocked with the behaviorur of the sales girl and they tried their best to give back the tax amount to her but, in vain. When your values are strong, you're respected automatically.

ETHICS — IN FICTION?

One management student went to the library and started searching for a book on ethics in management. After two hours of searching,, he was not able to find the book. The librarian who was observing this student called him and asked what he was looking for. Then the student replied, "I am looking for a book on ethics in management." Then Librarian replied, "Oh! You are looking for a book on ethics, it is not available in management section but it will be available in fiction."

Ethics From Childhood

When we look at the comments of IIM Ahedabad director regarding CAT scam, he observed that the scam was due to lack of ethics. Ethics should be taught not at post graduation level, but at the lower lever so that they could practise. He is right, because a PG student has already built up his values and attitude and he will not change by studying ethics as a paper at PG level. If you look into primitive education system, a Guru used to teach the concepts with moral stories, which inculcates the right value systems in them automatically at the right age. Now, there are no moral stories, no value system in nursery. My daughter, always complains that one teacher is regularly absent and never corrects homework, etc. One day, I asked her which subject that particular teacher takes and to my surprise the answer was 'moral sciences'.

MUNNAABHAI VS. MUNNA BHAI

Entrepreneurship LESSONS TO BE LEARNT........

"Excellence is an art won by training and habituation. We do not act rightly because we have virtue or excellence, but rather we have those because we have acted rightly. We are what we repeatedly do. Excellence, then, is not an act but a habit." – Aristotle

It is very interesting to know that Doctors in London had a special show on the movie "Munnabhai MBBS". There should be something special to learn for entrepreneurs in that particular film. Generally, doctors look into the **heart** where as entrepreneurs look into the **heart capital**.

One interesting question in the classroom arises is which functional management is more important? Marketing? Finance? or Human Resource? or Production??? Another interesting question is which level of management is important/ and who is most important in the organisation? Answer to all these questions is available in these two movies.

Generally, we think that the contribution from lowest the level is not much important and one can easily handle them. But, each one of them is important and different. Dealing with "people" is the toughest job that any entrepreneur faces. You ask any entrepreneur/boss he will give lectures on how tough it is to deal with the people. But, the Munnabhai and Munnabhai had shown the way to deal with tough people also, I hope all of you might be remembering the scene in which where Murali (Sunjay Dutt in Munnabhai MBBS) handles the sweeper in the hospital. The sweeper is used to shout in high pitch with everybody and Munnabhai had a solution for that. He recognized his work and highlights how significant cleanliness is to the hospital and offers the due credit to the sweeper. **The lessons for entrepreneurs are you can handle anybody with a smile, recognize the work and praise the people.**

"Strive to be the first: first to nod, first to smile, first to compliment, and first to forgive."

– Anonymous

If you praise people, they will rise above their level and contribute to the organization. **Give then the credit**. Manytimes, an entrepreneur takes the entire credit for himself for the success. Of course, he makes the employees responsible for failures. Though it is known to everyone, it is still worth recollecting it. Informal relationships are more powerful than formal relationships. Entrepreneurs should build informal relationship with their subordinates than formal relationships. (Some of you may not accept this because you would have had some bad experience where some of the subordinates had taken undue advantage of your informal relationship). Just think how many of them have done to you like this? Definitely, it might be 20 out of 100?. Then, why should you treat the remaining 80 so the same? **Keep smiling, keep recognizing, keep giving the credit, respect and identify them as the most important people to the organization so that they feel that they are empowered to contribute to the organization whole heartedly.**

The following incident happened in Japan. In a FMCG company, absentism is high among the drivers. When the management looked into the problems, they realized that they felt that they were not important to the organization and they are not properly treated in the organisation. But for a marketing company, supplying the product to the customer in the right time is very important and drivers are also a part of the value chain. Management called them and explained how each one of them was important to the organization and gave a uniform. To everybody's surprise, absentism among the drivers came down sharply and they started talking good about the company. ***There's good in everybody. Boost. Don't knock.*** The well-known success mantra is **'give respect and take respect.'**

This success formula is reflected in the part II of Munnabhai which is more popular because of Gandhigiri.

How to select the right employee?

Recently this incident happened in Bangalore. One company selected a candidate for marketing job as marketing executive after six rounds of selection process. The candidate was supposed to join in the next week. The Company manager decided to give a treat to the new colleague and invited him for dinner. The selected candidate went to the dinner and had a heated arguments with the waiter, spoke rashly and unnecessarily and they completed the dinner and went home. The next day, to his surprise he received a letter from the company stating that he was not selected. The company manager thought that if this is his behaviour and if he continues with the same behaviour with the customers tomorrow, what would be the fate of the company. Because, he knows that the cost of losing a customer is very high. According to one estimate, one customer will cost 10 million rupees. the figure is not exaggerated because we are speaking about the customer life cycle and gains and losses by his referrals also.

In the same context, one can observe that when a girl asked some help regarding the selection of her groom and it is very tough to judge a person within 10 or 15 minutes. Munnabhai says to observe the behaviour of the person in the hotel with the waiter, regarding how he calls the waiter. Unluckily, the candidate calls the waiter ...sshh ....sshh.. ssshh. And the girl takes the right decision.

Kind words do not cost much. Yet they accomplish much.

It is easy to judge the character of a person by analyzing not the way how he deals with superiors but with his subordinates.

Do not Compromise on Values

It is very interesting to observe Gandhigiri solutions to deal with the corruption: All might have observed the way a retired person gets the pension sanctioned without paying the bribe. Here is an interesting story about the Tatas. When they wanted to take-up the construction of the International Airport in Bangalore, they had made all the ground work and got selected in the bidding also. But, a political leader was asking some money to grant the permission to start the work. But Tatas were not ready because throughout the life of the company, they never bribed anybody. Even though, they had already invested some money and time on this project, (which will be in crore of rupees), they dropped the project to stick to their values. Instead of leaving the project they should have thought of some other alternative, may be Gandhigiri. Management lesson: **be creative in thinking.**

"One kind word can warm three winter months."

– Japanese Proverb

Everybody wants to become a leader but nobody wants to become a good follower. If you are not a good follower how can you expect to become good a leader? Now we will talk about the superiors or bosses. The biggest problem is with their ego. All problems can be solved except ego related problems. One might observe in the movie that how tough it is to say sorry to their friends with whom they are living together for quite a long period of time. How many bosses or superiors will put their ego down and say sorry to their subordinates when they have made a mistake? **If boss accepts the mistakes, subordinates also accept the mistakes in future and will not look for reasons**. In the film, when Gandhi asked Murali to say sorry to Circuit, you can observe how uncomfortable was Murali (LRM).

Love your Employees: Employees will Love your Organisation and Customers

These movies are about 'give respect and take respect' from one angle. Give love, the love will come back to you from another. If this concept of love is inculcated among the employees, the success is sure for any organisation. Generally, in any organisation only 40% of employees know the work and will work with heart, another 30% know the work but will not work, and the remaining 30% do not know how to work and will not work Just imagine **how successful will be your organisation if all of them put their heart and work for the organisation.**

Succession planning: Many big successful companies are struggling for succession planning, i.e., how to find the right leader for their companies in the near future. I think to some extent this movie will be helpful to find their successor. The successor should be not only competent but also should have high values and broader thinking of the large stakeholders of the company including society. We have heard of the product life cycle, industrial life cycle, customer life cycle but not best practices life cycle. In the longer run, here is my view of the best practices life cycle.

We started our practices from Gandhigiri (introduction) and then went to corruptgiri (growth stage) and then to dadagiri (maturity stage) and may die into chaos stage (decline stage). Then, as there is a re launching of the PLC, or ILC and we may start with Gandhigiri and then again proceed. Gandhigiri may not restart immediately but in another 15 to 25 years it may start; now we can observe the symptoms. If all the young generations practise Gandhigiri, good days are not far away.

"We must be the part of the change we wish to see in the world."

– M.K. Gandhi

Importance of the first impression: If somebody is looking from marketing point of view (Customer Relationship Management point of view), there is a lesson too: **The first impression:** When Murali enters FM Studio to talk with an anchor, he greets her and talks with her without knowing that the she is in soundproof room. Then, he is back to the toilet and mentions about the first impression. One should learn that there is no second chance to get the first impression with customers/employees.

Without mentioning certain important lively incidents in both the movies, it is incomplete. The first one is regarding a patient (considered as a subject in the movie, i.e., who never responds to stimuli). When all the doctors lost hope on this patient, Munnabhai cured him with **heart,** and not with the medicine. We should believe that many health disorders are more psychological in nature than physiological. It is the right time to recollect Maslow's need hierarchy theory, which speaks about psychological and physiological needs. Indeed the power of physical needs is persuasive (We read in the newspaper that somebody was killed for just 10 rupees or for some little food etc.). But the power of psychological needs is unknown, and it is enduring and unlimited. In the organizations, many times we come across a situation where salaries are hiked but productivity is not commensurately improved much. For those organizations it is time to concentrate on psychological needs rather than physiological needs. The important concept to be observed is the power of love. Doctors treat the patient as a subject but Munnabhai looks at him from the human point of view with love and affection. I hope all of you know the results at the end of the day. The same concept is applicable even in the organizations. Love your employees; employees in turn will love your organisation and the customers. In Gandhiji's words, love is the strongest force the world possesses. Entrepreneurs should make use of this force.

The second one is about a doctor's father (Paappu) who is mad about playing carom. Paappu was brought to the hospital because he stopped taking food for the last few days. All doctors started treating him from the medical point of view but Munnabhai had shown the way. The lesson for the entrepreneurs is **"don't give what you want to give, but give what others want to take."** Give the employees what they require rather than what you want to give. May be a little more of respect, care, love, etc.... Don't think that money will be propelling force!. One might have observed the power of love and human relations in the MBBS movie when all the employees of the hospital revolt against the M.D. including his daughter for the sake of Munnabhai.

SECOND INNINGS HOUSE

Even if you're not an employee or employer of any organisation still there is a lesson for you as a human being in LRM. Priyanka runs a home for elders the "second innings house." I do want to recollect the happiness of a father when his son was brought to his birthday (of course, forcefully). Parents do not expect anything but a little love and care.

If there can be a second innings house for the parents, there can be second innings relationships in the organisation also. If you had poor relations with the employees, still you can begin with a positive attitude to build good relations. One must not forget that employees go by action rather than words. Actions speak louder than words. Just imagine your boss comes to your house to attend your daughter's birthday. Of course, you will be delighted. Similarly, if you attend your subordinates' functions in their homes, they will also be delighted. Give a small helping hand to the employees when they are in trouble. Many entrepreneurs say that they are always helpful to the employees when they are in trouble as far as the rules permit. It is like asking the patient to fill the form before joining the hospital irrespective of his condition, which you have seen in MBBS. But, the right concept here is to go beyond the rules and help them. Then, employees also go beyond their considerations and contribute to the organisation. Send a greeting card to the employees on their birthdays, wish them on their marriage days, visit their homes, send the company vehicle to all the employees when they stay back for completion of work, conduct small birthday parties in the office, conduct some site visits, generate some enthusiasm among the employees. For example, give a surprise gift to the employee for the best suggestion for improvement, talk to the employees with a smile and so on which may go a long way in building meaningful relationships. Please keep in mind that tough decisions need not be told harshly. The greatest success mantra not only in organizations, but also in human relations is 'give **respect and take respect'.** (Beyond that is give respect and give respect). We know it, but let us follow it now in spirit. **Treat your employees as your mother treats you. Thus you are building a winning organisation. Because nothing can match a mother's heart.**

There are many strategies as to how to select the right candidate for the job. But, no strategy is available to select the right organisation. Do not join in those companies where your employers had not taken sufficient care about his/her parents. Because when he/she cannot take care about his/her parents, how can he take care of his/her employees.

In the selection process, find out whether a candidate loves his/her parents (takes sufficient care and show love towards parents and what is their status). If the candidate does not take care of his/her parents, do not select him because a person who does not love his/her parents who had given everything to him cannot love his organisation too.

The Power of "CAN"

We really underestimated the power of "CAN". If you look into LRM, all of us never thought the problems 'can' be solved through Gandhigiri. But, the movie has demonstrated it; we can do it better with the help of Gandhigiri. The motive behind it is definitely the CAN. **If you think you can, you can do it, if you think you can't, you can't do it.**

The entire marketing is dependent on one success mantra which is given by Mahatma Gandhi which is displayed in the banks. Many bank employees think that it is for the customers but not for them. Of course, all of us know about it. but very few will practise it: It is right time to recollect it.

"Who is a customer?

A customer is the most important person ever in our company—

A customer is not dependent on us but we are dependent on him.

"A customer is not an interruption on our work; He is the purpose of it. We are not doing him a favour by serving him; he is doing us a favour by giving us the opportunity to do so. A customer is not some one to argue, to match wits with; no body ever won an argument with a customer. A customer is a person who brings his wants — it is our job to handle them profitability to him and to ourselves."

— Mahatma Gandhi

"Where there is a Love, there is a Life."

How to get love: There is a small lesson for the teenagers who look for love in the movie LRM. Gandhiji asks Munnabhai to tell the truth (as he is not professor to) Priyanka to get the love from her in the long run. Many times, to cover up one lie we have to tell more lies. That can be avoided by being honest from the starting. This is applicable in organisation also.

GET WELL SOON is the right strategy to justify the Gandhigiri. The way in which the house is got back is an eye opener to all.

The motto of Gandhigiri is if you are strong in values you will never be defeated. Last, but not the least, both the movies are about love, human relations, and Gandhigiri which is not only relevant to the organisation, but also to all of us as human beings. **In the words of Gandhi. "nonviolence is a weapon of the strong."**

Gandhigiri is not an end, it is only the **beginning**.

Conclusion..... the beginning

After going through this book, great challenges are: How to possess so many qualities at the same time? Which is the most important? How to take right decisions? Is there any short cut method for entrepreneurship? Entrepreneurship is more like swimming. You cannot sit at the bank and plan to win a race. You should jump into water and enjoy the fight.

If an entrepreneur thinks and acts like this mother, many problems are easily solved.

In a small village, there lived the family of a mother and her son. The son had lost his father at a tender age and the mother was his sole caretaker. Years passed by and the son grew up. He met a beautiful girl and fell in love. When they decided to marry, the girl laid down a condition that she would marry him only if he handed over his mother's heart to her. The boy was taken aback. He went home in a dejected mood. The mother found that something was worng and enquired. He hesitantly narrated the girl's demand. She said, "I can give anything for you, my son. Take my heart and live happily with your loved one." The boy was happy and rushed to the girl with his mother's heart in his hands. But, he slipped on the way and he fell down. The mother's heart said, "Son, be careful, I hope nothing happened to you, take care. If something happens to you I will feel unhappy." This is how a mother loves her children.

If entrepreneurs can think and act like a mother, many qualities which are mentioned in the previous chapters will follow automatically. They must address emotional issues of all stakeholders with sensitivity and consideration.

Entrepreneurship is a continuous learning process. Learning might be from the past experience also. Average men learn from their own mistakes, while intelligent ones learn from other mistakes. Learning from experience, however, can be complicated. It can be much more difficult to learn from success than from failure. If we fail, we are careful in future. Success can indiscriminately reinforce all our prior actions. Intelligent people learn from others, success too.

Do you think you lack some of the competencies like technological, marketing, financial, etc which hinder you?. Sometimes the lack of skill creates an entrepreneurial opportunity. A Jobless man applied for the position of 'office boy' at Microsoft. The HR manager interviewed him and then watched him cleaning the floor as a test.

'You are hired, he said. Give me your e-mail address and I'll send you the application to fill in, as well as date when you may start. The man replied, 'But I don't have a computer, neither an email.'

'I'm sorry', said the HR manager. If you don't have an e-mail, that means you do not exist. And he who does not exist, cannot have a job.'

The man was desperate with only $10 in his pocket. He then decided to go to the supermarket and buy a 10Kg tomato.

He then sold the tomatoes going from door to door. In less than two hours, he succeeded in doubling his capital. He repeated the operation three times, and returned home with $60. He realized that he can survive this way. Thus, his money doubled or tripled everyday. Shortly, he bought a cart, then a truck, and then he had his own fleet of delivery vehicles. Five years later, the man was one of the biggest food retailers in the US. He started to plan his family's future, and decided to buy insurance. He called an insurance agent, and chose a protection plan.

When the agreement was concluded, the agent wanted his email.

The man replied, I don't have an e-mail.' The agent was curious, 'You don't have an email, and yet have succeeded in building an empire. Can you imagine what you could have been if you did have an e-mail?' The man thought for a while and replied, 'Yes, I would have been an office boy at Microsoft!'

Technical skills are only a part of the life of an entrepreneur.

Many a times, we say that because of some other people we are not able to become entrepreneurs. Even in the organizations also, we feel that our growth is restricted by somebody else. For all those, who feel that their growth is restricted by somebody else the following story will be an eye opener.

One day, when the employees reached the office saw the following notice: 'Yesterday, the person who has been hindering your growth in this company passed away. We invite you to join the funeral in the gym room.

In the beginning, they all got sad for the death of one of their colleagues, but after a while they were curious to know who was that man who hindered the growth of his and his colleagues and the company itself.

The excitement in the gym was such that security agents were ordered to control the crowd. The more people reached the coffin, the more the excitement was. Everyone thought: 'Who is this guy who was hindering my progress? Well, at last he died!'. One by one shocked employees got closer to the coffin, and when they looked inside it, they suddenly became speechless. They stood nearby the coffin, shocked in silence, as if someone had touched the deepest part of their soul. There was a mirror inside the coffin: There was also a sign next to the mirror:

'There is only one person who is capable to set limits to your growth: it is YOU. You are the only person who can revolutionize your life. You are the only person who can influence your happiness, your realization and your success. You are the only person who can help yourself.,

Your life does not change when your **boss changes**, when your friends change, when your parents change, when your partner changes, or when your **company changes.** Your life changes when YOU change, when you go beyond your limiting beliefs, when you realize that you are the only one responsible for your life.

'The most important relationship you can have is the one you have with yourself.' Examine yourself, watch yourself. Don't be afraid of difficulties, impossibilities and losses, be a winner, build yourself and your dreams.

It's the way you face life and that makes the difference!

For every beginning, there is an end and for every ending, there is a beginning. Entrepreneurship is also like that. It is a continuous, dynamic and challenging process. If you want to create wealth, the only way is through entrepreneurship.

❑ ❑ ❑

REFERENCES

1. Entrepreneurship: by Vasant Desai
2. Entrepreneurship: Kanka
3. Project Management: Prasanna Chandra
4. www.sander.com
5. www.lijjathpappad.com
6. www.southwestairlines.com
7. www.dubbawala.com